Growing Up
in an
Amish-Jewish Cult

Book Two

Deception

Patricia Hochstetler

Growing Up in an Amish-Jewish Cult

Book Two
Deception

BAKER TRITTIN PRESS
Winona Lake, Indiana

Growing Up in an Amish-Jewish Cult / Book Two, Deception
By Patricia Hochstetler

Printed in the United States of America
Cover Design: Paul S. Trittin
Back Cover Photos: Mike Albin
Published by Baker Trittin Press
P.O. Box 277
Winona Lake, Indiana 46590

To order additional copies please call (574) 269-6100
or email info@btconcepts.com
http://www.bakertrittinpress.com

Publishers Cataloging-Publication Data
Patricia Hochstetler, 1948-
     Growing Up in an Amish-Jewish Cult / Book Two, Deception
     Patricia Hochstetler - Winona Lake, Indiana
     Baker Trittin Press, 2007

        p.   cm.

Library of Congress Control Number: 2007939004
ISBN 10: 0-9787316-5-4
ISBN 13: 978-0-9787316-5-6
     1. Autobiography 2. Religious 3. Christian
     I. Title   II. Growing Up in an Amish-Jewish Cult /
     Book Two, Deception
BIO18000

                              Second Printing

Acknowledgments

The following individuals contributed to the *Growing Up in an Amish-Jewish Cult* trilogy. This book, the previous one and the book to follow, which took over one painful decade to write, is the release of a childhood of caged thoughts now unshackled and put into a labor of concern for others.

I must acknowledge all of the Lael Colony members who shared their experiences with me and lived out the drama and endured its confusion with me. May God bless all of you!

This book would not have been written and edited without the patience and support of my husband, Ezra, my children and grandchildren, my friends, and church family.

I thank my editor, Dr. Marvin G. Baker, who stayed with me in prayer and deed thoughout the grueling process of editing this book, and my publication advisor and publisher, Paul Trittin, who offered continuous support, guidance, and encouragement. They were outstanding in their dedication to bring the dangers of cults to the attention of the public.

I also humbly thank the public, especially the people of my roots, the Amish, for their support of my first book, *Delusion*, which was received far beyond my expectations. Thank you to all of my reviewers, website helpers, and those who helped in any way.

Mostly I thank my Lord Jesus Christ, who with love, mercy, and grace, spared my life and delivered me from despair.

Table of Contents

Patricia Hochstetler

Preface

This book continues our dark journey into the life of a young girl totally isolated from any world beyond a small Tennessee valley and the vast cotton fields of a Mississippi plantation. We find her Garden of Eden turned into a prison camp of child labor and captured souls. *Delusion* began with the great dreams of personal salvation under the guidance of their "great" man, The Elder. In *Deception* we encounter the reality of The Elder's burdensome rules and the messages he claimed to bring directly from God which finally strangled the humanity of every colony member. The joys of Paradise have gradually metamorphosed into the endless pains of an earthly Hell. Still they hoped for salvation.

How can this be? How can such good people who are committed to Christ find themselves so helplessly lost in another man's egocentric nightmare? How can parents bear to watch their children suffer and even die and still show no emotion? How can a child born in a Christian home live 12 years of her childhood without ever hearing "I love you" cross the lips of her parents, family, or church? How could she go through her childhood and never hear music, other than the voice of birds? Was this really what these good parents set off to give their children? NO!

They set off to give their children the assurance of God's salvation through Jesus Christ. They set off to surround their children with the *love* and support of a cohesive Christian community. They set off to assure their children of the reality of God's *love*. What they got instead was deception in its most tragic form. Their tragedy was that these parents soon became conduits of this same deception.

What does this have to do with me, you, or our friends? Perhaps a great deal. Here is a tale of Christian families not much different than our own, caught up in the dreams of spiritual perfection as taught by their "great" man. Do we dare see any of our own spiritual tendancies in this tale? Are we ever tempted to take the easy way out and answer to the call of a "great" man rather than prove his words with the Words of God Himself, the Bible? If we are, we yield to it at our own peril and the peril of our children and our children's children.

Not only does the all powerful personality of a "great" man split the universal body of the Church, but it creates the deception which may plague generations to come with a faith based on his ego rather than a faith based on the Word of God alone. Of course we all may interpret His Word slightly differently, but we should never permit a "great" man's twisting or omissions, minimizing or additions to dictate our faith. As many in Lael Colony eventually learned, there is no last word but the Word of God itself. No NEW Church can be founded on the divine revelations of God to one "great" man, and then have it passed down from one generation to the next until it is all the people know.

Yes, what Patricia Hochstetler is calling us to be diligent for is our defense against the beauty of any "great" man and his cult. The neutralization Gospel purity by the temptations of another man's dream can only lead to the spiritual deception and death of everyone who follow's his call.

Without the formal education most of us enjoy, Patricia Hochstetler has taken up her pen to call each of us to remain true to our Lord, remain with a strong company of believers, and test each doctrine with the Word of God. In spite of our several doctrinal differences, numerous congregational traditions, and countless personal walks with Christ, we are all one in Him. We must do all we can to protect that truth within ourselves and those we love.

Paul S. Trittin
Publisher

Chapter 1

Who Is
The Elder?

Delusion is a serious charge. It is defined as a psychotic belief that persists in spite of indisputable evidence to the contrary. Mack Sharky was responsible for deluding the truth-seeking Amish who settled near Aberdeen, Mississippi.

Three vital needs for a child's security are honesty, consistency, and love. All three were missing from the life and teachings of Mack Sharky, the self-proclaimed Elder. Deception, the practice of deliberately deceiving, was demonstrated in a most stark manner in a conversation concerning his 'Nazarite' position. According to Sharky a Nazarite kept *every* day as a Sabbath and did no physical labor.

My aunt posed a hypothetical question to The Elder. "If a six month old baby in a crib was in a burning house, would you go in and rescue that baby?"

He responded, "No! Because of my Nazarite position, I could not carry anything through a doorway. Therefore it would be impossible for me to carry any child from a burning house."

His comment was a closely kept secret, but those who heard it from my aunt wouldn't believe her. However it was enough to deter her and her immediate family from following Sharky.

Deception and delusion are so very subtle. Innocent, naïve, and trusting individuals in search of truth are vulnerable. These sincere Amish families in Aberdeen, Mississippi, were willing to listen to — and follow — someone they thought to be knowledgeable in the Bible.

A Scripture reciting, charismatic, persuasive individual was lurking to capture these hungry souls.

Who was The Elder that came looking for them? That's still a mystery! He freely admitted changing his name several times. He often announced, "Nobody really knows who I am!" Six times, in his twenty-three year path with the Lael Colony members, his followers were ordered to address him by a different name. Most in the colony were willing to just call him The Elder.

In 1946 when Mack Sharky first hitchhiked to the quiet Amish group in Aberdeen, he appeared to be in his fifties. His black felt stovepipe hat accentuated his six foot tall, thin frame and its 160 pounds. The Elder always walked erect and alert. He projected a sense of humility as he placed his arms behind his back and gripped one hand with the other. His hands looked soft, unlike a working man's hands.

He had salt and pepper, grayish hair, and he neatly tucked his beard and his hair inside his shirt collar. His ears stayed hidden under big, puffy, course, long hair. Few wrinkles were visible on his fair skin. His long, narrow nose had a distinct hump in it. His blue eyes showed friendliness, yet was accompanied by a blank expression. Words squeezed out from between his thin lips which gapped enough to show his decaying and missing teeth. The corners of his mouth neither turned up nor down with expression. His soft-spoken words were well put together in English.

From the very beginning his power was unmistakable. The Elder schmoozed his way into the Amish homes and then stayed. "God blesses people like you who provide for His servant," he often said.

The Elder always wore black, corduroy pants and jacket, a pilgrim-gray, twill shirt, black socks, shoes, and felt hat. He requested his jacket be trimmed with a dark, navy blue ribbon. When offered a straw hat for daily use, The Elder said, "That's a work hat. I only wear a black felt, dress hat."

Seeming to have a photographic memory, The Elder wooed the Amish with his superior Bible knowledge and memorization. He answered the *why* questions by saying, "I was called in 1937 to serve God. I am a Nazarite, a servant of God and an apostle of God. God speaks to me. I have taken the vow of a Nazarite as in Numbers 6 for the rest of my life. I cannot cut my hair or beard. I eat no grapes, drink no wine, or partake of anything from grapes. I am a holy man that keeps every day as a Sabbath. Therefore I cannot ever work or carry anything in or out of any house or building."

His knowledge of the Old Testament rituals and traditions was convincing. Who among these meek Amish believers dared challenge someone with such a command of biblical teachings and history? He claimed to know Yiddish although we never heard him speak the language. He had a good command of English, but he never showed interest in learning Pennsylvania Dutch, a language common among his followers.

More things leaked from The Elder's lips as time passed.

"My parents were Orthodox Jews and not originally from the United States of America," The Elder shared. "They spoke Yiddish, and they had some connections with the Ukraine. I am an Orthodox Jew from the lineage of Joseph and tribe of Judas."

Some even wondered if it were possible that his family members had escaped from Hitler's camps. The Elder never revealed his parent's names. He claimed that he was the middle of nine children and the first born in the United States. He never disclosed the date or place of his birth. He claimed to have a younger sister named Ellen who at one time lived in Akron, Ohio. He also spoke of his brother, Bill Sharky, who lived in Pennsylvania.

In unguarded moments he spoke of his earlier years. "I had a car and drove in my younger years, and I worked on the railroad . . . I knew more and worked harder and faster than anybody around me . . . I'm well traveled . . . I jumped on trains and rode coast to coast, and I hitchhiked much of my traveling years . . . At times I slept in cardboard boxes to stay warm . . . I was an electrician in Pennsylvania, and I gave my mother all my checks . . . I stayed with her and took care of her till she died . . . During that time my brother, Bill, kept asking me if and when I was going to start running after women."

Most of the time The Elder appeared like a quiet, docile man and stayed to himself. He maintained an air of mystery. Some in our colony questioned if The Elder was a eunuch from birth or otherwise. That too remains a mystery. This man knew about sexuality but didn't show any personal interest.

On different occasions it appeared he enjoyed speaking of his prison experiences.

With his arms crossed at the chest he would place his right index finger on his lips and then with it stroke his mustache from side to side as he appeared to be thinking. Then with his right hand he would stroke his chin and gray beard downward as he spoke.

"I learned much of the Bible while imprisoned," he began, "and I know it cover to cover . . . In prison I once fasted for forty days and forty nights because they would not serve kosher food according to the Jewish tradition and my requests . . . During the depression I was picked up on the streets for vagrancy and curfew violations . . . Remember not all prisoners are bad people."

His self-effacement and humility belied his desire for power and unquestioned loyalty. His deception about the simplicity of his commands proved to be mind-boggling.

After he had garnered his followers, he began with only one simple order: keep The Golden Rule, Matthew 7:12. He stressed that for quite some time. Then he even allowed the people to see doctors. Later he added The Ten Commandments, Deuteronomy 5:6-12, but he had one exception for "Thou shalt not kill." He ordered us to kill all snakes because they represented the Devil. This first peculiar order gave the people something to study.

It was not long before The Elder announced a revolutionary idea. The people would, like him, eat no pork. They were to sell all their pigs and live according to the dietary laws presented in chapter 23 of Leviticus.

Who is The Elder?

"You must see no evil, hear no evil, or say no evil," The Elder ordered. "Turn your back if you see bad things, plug your ears if something sounds bad, and bite your lips and keep them sealed. If necessary, bite your tongue so you say as little as possible. You must not laugh, cry, or be foolish," he commanded. "At all times keep your face from being an open book."

The Elder ordered us to keep his ever increasing rules and to be sober and vigilant for the adversary, the Devil, is as a roaring lion walking about seeking to devour us. "These rules I give you are not my rules. They are God's rules. God speaks to me, His servant, and you must listen," The Elder declared. "God wants His people perfect, and in this way we can all know what He wants. If you do wrong, I will refer to you as being in the 'red' because red is a bad color. Red represents the Devil. You must strive to be God's perfect people.

"I also ban wearing anything red, purple, or scarlet in color. Those colors are for harlots," he announced. In succeeding days he added yellow, pink, green and many other colors to this list. *Why couldn't we wear green? Is green like the grass and trees that God made bad? And what about brown like the soil? Why is brown bad? Why? What about the yellow and orange flowers on our garden vegetables, are they bad?*

The Elder banned all colony members from planting any flowers in our yards or gardens. *Why? Are flowers really evil? Why do the bees make such good honey from flowers, and we can eat it? Why isn't the honey evil? Where does it say in the Bible that flowers are evil?*

The Elder's instructions continued. "You shall not buy a dog according to what the King James Bible says in Deuteronomy 23:18. Always bury dead things and your dung. Don't leave anything filthy around. Don't lay up any riches. Money is the root of all evil." The Elder went on to shout, "I command that only the fathers have money and handle that filthy lucre. No wife and no child shall have any money in their procession."

The Elder would never touch any money. He left that

to others, but he insisted on control. Any money the colony received had to be touched by only one of the fathers because The Elder did not want to contaminate us or himself. Even when he traveled, he carried no money. He was an artful beggar.

The Elder ordered, "Stay poor and humble before God. Memorize the Bible as fast as possible. If anyone ever asks if you have a Bible, take no thought for your life. Answer yes. If they spare your life but take your Bible, they cannot take God's Word from you if it's hidden in your heart."

He ordered that we first learn all the books in the Old Testament and then all those in the New Testament. After that was memorized we were to learn all the headings for each chapter. He called them scripture lines. We were to know them by heart by the time we were eleven, so we could find anything in the Bible quickly. We were to learn the "nine blocks" of scriptures that he had chosen for us to memorize. (See Appendix) I tried hard to learn all of these scriptures.

The Elder advised us to work hard and set high goals. Eventually he banned doctors, dentists, and all medications. He declared that God is the great healer. People who became ill were to lay in pain until they felt better or died. They suffered toothaches until their teeth rotted and fell out. Broken bones were never set. They healed as God allowed. Injuries were treated with salt water and wrappings. Cataracts, injury to the eyes, or failing vision due to age were left to 'whatever God allowed.'

"God will heal you if he wants," The Elder proclaimed. "He is God. He — not man — determines life, health, and death."

The Elder had instructions about strangers too. "Follow my example, hide from strangers whenever you can. If you are outside, step behind a tree, building, or anything or go inside a barn or the house wherever to keep from being seen. If you are in the cotton field when a stranger appears, keep your heads down in the cotton stalks and keep picking as fast as you can. If you are hoeing and the cotton stalks are small, keep your heads down low so your face will not show.

Hoe rapidly down the row to get away from them. If you must be seen, make sure you're voice is not heard. Seal your lips and don't talk. If they insist, say 'ask my father.'

"Avoid the heathens as much as possible so you won't hear or see evil. Don't say any evil words like the heathen, worldly people do. Refrain from worldly words like love."

Such deception! This teaching totally missed the message of God's love, the central point of Jesus Christ whom he professed to serve.

"Don't wonder about what is in the world," The Elder declared. "Ignore it. Don't even say 'Oh, boy.' That's like calling for a partner. It's not becoming for women who claim celibacy. Refrain from saying, 'Oh, my goodness' because it sounds like you think you're good. God is good not you."

His directions defied logic, but no one challenged him. "When praying, face the north. When bowing down for the floor prayers, point your head toward the north and your feet will point south toward the Devil. If you are unable to face north, then face east. Never face south toward the Devil to pray or sleep. Put all your beds with the head to the north so when you sleep, your head is toward God and not the Devil. Don't face your outhouse door north or south. Face outhouses east first and if not east, face them west.

"I will change your names as God orders. I'll tell you His commands and what to do and not do. Obey God's words if you want to live long on this earth and be blessed." The Elder ordered, "Only read and learn from the King James Version of the Bible, but you can keep your German Bibles. I will instruct you to underline certain scriptures in all your Bibles. Make sure to underline all of them for these are important verses. Remember there shall be no complaining in our midst as the Israelites did or God will punish you. Obey God's commandments."

The Elder had opinions about animals too. "Remember that snakes are bad and represent the Devil and evil. Birds are good and stand for good things."

This left no room for asking any questions that passed through my mind. *What about the blue ribbon on men's clothing in Numbers 15:38-41? What about the animal sacrifices? Baptism? And all the other 'why' questions I had.*

I wondered why The Elder often spoke of the holocaust and Hitler. He seemed to be obsessed with the book titled *The Black Book, Nazi Crimes against the Jewish People,* published in 1946, by The Jewish Black Book Committee. Adults claimed this book unfit for children to read. I only saw its cover and wished to know what was inside.

The Elder predicted the end of the world two times, once while we were in Tennessee and once in Mississippi. I couldn't understand why he had us prepare for the end of the world, but then it didn't happen. Why? The Elder had no explanations. This was puzzling to me. If God talked to The Elder, why didn't he know for sure? Was this another test of faith or was this some spiritual thing that us carnal people couldn't understand? I didn't know why and couldn't find out why. Life went on with the same routine year after year after year.

Why did The Elder keep *every day* as a Sabbath when he instructed us to keep only Saturday as the Sabbath? He ordered that we keep the Sabbath as in Leviticus 23:3 and according to his added rules. During my childhood in the colony we observed every Saturday, the seventh day of the week, as our Sabbath. We worked in the fields or went to school Sunday through Friday. We referred to the Sabbath as the Lord's Day, a holy day of rest. We followed The Elder's modified Jewish instructions just as he ordered.

"Keep the Sabbath holy as unto the Lord," The Elder constantly reminded us. "Before sunset, everybody must bathe and put on their best clean clothes and wear only those on the Sabbath Day. Prepare all Sabbath meals and food, wood stove fires, and oil lamps before sundown Friday. You may add wood to the stoves if the wood is in the house and near the stove before sunset. Pick up no wood, sticks, or anything outside on the Sabbath. Light no fires on the Sabbath. If the stove fire goes out, you will be cold. If the lamps go out, you sit in the dark. Do not carry anything through a doorway. Don't carry one thing in or out of your house – not even a Bible. Don't carry anything in your pockets except a handkerchief and Bible verses, and they must be placed in the pocket before sundown. This is the day to rest only. Focus on The Lord. Learn His word, and worship Him.

"To honor and be faithful to The Lord, we will have Sabbath meetings from one to four or five o'clock in the afternoon," The Elder announced. "When I'm not around either traveling or caught up in the clouds like Elijah and gone to heaven, each family is to read five Bible chapters in the afternoon. You always keep all Sabbath days holy. Remember Exodus 20:8 says to keep the Sabbath day"

The Sabbath meetings were first held in homes and later in the schoolhouse. The meetings began at one o'clock and lasted until four or five. The Elder was the only one who spoke, and we had to listen every moment to what he was saying. His piercing blue eyes quieted the restless. He quoted long passages from the King James Bible, the only permissible translation. Was this because it was the most difficult translation for us Amish to understand?

After the meetings moved to the schoolhouse, I recall The Elder saying, "I will communicate with God." It seemed to me he often stood quietly for a long time, arms rolled up on his chest. His right hand was raised and his index finger covered the middle of his lips as he stroked his mustache from side to side and then his beard downward. In this pose he walked to the back of the room behind us and stood by the stove looking up for long periods of time. When he came forward, he shared his new thought. He began doing this more often as time went on, with long silent times at the meetings.

Some believe The Elder had tried to become like a Russian mystic. To that end he learned the Bible cover to cover. He had found a group willing to follow him and to keep him for the rest of his life.

Patricia Hochstetler

Chapter 2

My Family

When my parents, Clarence and Mary Long, decided to take their young children to join an Amish type group in Tennessee, they were leaving Indiana for one reason and one reason only. They were going to find something better for their children.

In the summer of 1952 my family traveled from Indiana to Tennessee, and a short distance off the scenic and historic Natchez Trace Parkway we entered Lael Colony. We made our new home on the colony's 2,005 acres. Swanegan Branch Road ran through the middle of the acreage. With a locked gate across the road on the north toward Colonwood and a locked gate on the south toward Iron City we were isolated from the world. Our new village lay in the middle of a timberland jungle and in a deep, wide, and moist valley walled in by a giant west hill and a very high east hill.

Welcomed by The Elder, his colony, and many of Mom's Amish family, we were happy to join them. What joy it seemed to be in Lael Valley and to have the privilege of becoming a part of Lael Colony — God's people on God's land flowing with milk and honey. Still this four-year-old child did wonder why we had to forget Elkhart, Indiana, everyone there, and everything that we knew before. But listening to the adults around me, I felt I was one step from heaven, and the atmosphere seemed to prove it. The people referred to the land as the Garden of Eden, their utopia, and claimed they were living in bliss.

The land was clothed with timber, threaded with sparkling, fresh creeks, and knotted with springs. I saw more land, woods, and water then I ever imagine existed. It seemed we were on a new earth or at least on the other side of the one we were on when we lived in Indiana. As a four-year-old, I listened to the whippoorwills and other birds and felt I was in paradise.

I overheard Grandpa say to Mom, *"Des himelich blatz iss von de Hawa.* (This heavenly place is from the Lord.)"

Grandpa Benjamin Miller had a pleasant look — a heart smile that I could sense — but it only surfaced once in awhile. He looked serious most of the time. A proven follower, he looked to others for guidance. The closest I felt to my *Grossfadda* (Grandpa) was at age four and five when we lived with them in Lael Valley and when he came to our home and had long talks with Mom. I can still see him outside under a shade tree talking to Mom. He stood there with one foot on the ground, the other foot up on the side of the tree and under his behind as a seat. There he sat on the heel of his shoe and leaned back on the trunk of the tree as if he had a complete chair. He alternated moving his foot from the tree to the ground and vice versa. Taking his straw hat from his head, he hung it on his knee that poked out from the tree. He talked Pennsylvania Dutch. When Grandpa tired, he sat on the ground or a block of wood. Mom listened while she worked.

I remember Grandpa praying and reading the Bible in English and sometimes in German. He often worked in the garden or field. He was a known sleepwalker. Once he got up at midnight, thinking it was early morning. He lit a kerosene lantern, went to the barn, and harnessed and hitched up his mules to plow. He awoke as he headed for the field and realized he was sleepwalking. He took the mules home and went back to bed. This story was repeated for years.

One thing I knew for sure. I did not ever want Grandpa to give me a switching because that's when his frail body grew into a huge figure. His blue eyes turned red, and his light brown hair stood on end as he took off his straw hat.

My Family

He knew how to humiliate with words and actions. He made the child getting the punishment or the person they had wronged pick the switch from a green tree. He surely knew how to use it like a whip. It was experience he learned from having thirteen living children. My mom was his second child, and he had one younger than I. Whenever we parted, Grandpa usually said, *"Sein goot! On dein mudda gehowda."* (Be good! And obey your mother.)

Grandpa Miller was the only grandpa I ever knew. My Grandpa Frank Wilbur Long saw me only once as a baby when my parents visited him in prison. He never saw me again nor I him. He died in prison before I left the cult.

Grandma Miller, Elizabeth (Amstutz), a vibrant, ambitious, courageous and friendly grandma seemed to get a lot done and still remain in a good mood. I enjoyed being around my *grossmudda* (grandma). She often strolled down the lane and across the creek to our home to visit Mom. They always spoke Pennsylvania Dutch, and I understood things I wasn't supposed to know. Once I overheard Mom and Grandma talking in low tones.

Mom interrupted to say, *"Sie kon nat howda vas meah sagochta, on sie kon nat alles fasta,"* (She can't hear what we say, and she can't understand all of it.)"

I never told them that I knew what they said. I kept a distance with a sharply tuned ear and learned a lot of things I was not supposed to know. It was entertaining and challenging for me to listen and learn.

One cool, fall morning, I remember Grandma walking to our home barefoot and hot as usual. She led Marlow, their billy goat. I ran to meet her and said, "Grandma, Marlow is peeing on your dress!"

"Oh! *Unfastanlick, Unfastanlick,"* (Unbelievable, Unbelievable,) Grandma said as she backed up quickly. "Marlow, *Nat so do!"* (Don't do that!)

I walked with them to our barnyard where Grandma put stinky Marlow. Grandma, worn out after walking Marlow, sat her fifty gallon drum size body down on a log and talked to Mom. Next time Grandma came, Benja tagged along. It was colder, but Grandma still didn't wear a coat or shoes because she was always warm. She sat on a log near the woodpile, and Benja, age three and her youngest, straddled the log and snuggled up beside her and put his hands under her armpit to warm them. I also straddled the log and snuggled up on the other side and put my hands under her other big, fat, warm armpit. What a nice heater! We would warm up, get down and run around till cold, and then go for her armpits again. She would then put her arms around us yet no hugs or kisses were allowed.

Once we moved to the cotton plantation Grandma never worked in the fields. She had too much to do caring for her family, and she was not in shape for that hard work or the heat in the cotton fields. I enjoyed going to her home with Mom and listening to them talk as they planted garden, fed or butchered chickens, or whatever. Grandma Miller was always special, very special.

The day Grandma Miller died felt like one of the saddest days of my life. Grandma was only 52, and I was fourteen. The separation The Elder had put between my family and hers stole joyful times from us. Nevertheless there was a fondness and living hope that we would be reunited and that never ended until her death. I always wished I could have had more years of joy with her. Now she was gone! I felt it couldn't be, but it was. Helpless and hopeless, life continued without her. She died in her favorite chair soon after the sun set on Friday evening.

Because it was the Sabbath, Grandpa wasn't allowed to make any arrangements or to do anything until the sun had set on Saturday evening. So they laid her on the floor in a hallway between the living room and bedrooms and covered her till the Sabbath ended. For nearly 24 hours she lay there. After the sunset on Saturday Grandpa walked to the plantation manager's house and told him that his wife had died.

The manager called the undertaker, and they came and took her body. Early the next morning, unlike with other deaths, the undertaker placed her open, homemade, wooden box at the grave side. The Elder was away hitchhiking, so the wooden box was opened long enough for all of us to have one, last, quick peek before a final farewell. No service or words were uttered. Once all the people filed by they put the top back on the box, nailed it shut, and lowered it into the grave. Grandpa, Dad, and the other men and boys covered the grave. We went home and nobody talked.

I very much liked — we couldn't say loved — my Grandma Miller, and it didn't seem fair for her to die so suddenly and so young. She had an asthma type problem but was never allowed to seek any medical help. I felt I would never get over missing Grandma Miller.

I always felt Grandma Miller was a perfect grandma in every way, and I wished I had more time with her, but it would never be. Now she had become another statistic. Now, two months after her sister Lydia's sudden death from a burst gallbladder and six years after Uncle David's bizarre death, she too was dead. Three lives cut short and buried young. We all wondered who would be next.

I couldn't help thinking about my Indiana Grandma Long. By now I didn't know if she was dead or alive. I was told not to even think of her, but I couldn't stop. The Elder had declared her a heathen, of the Devil, wicked, and of the world. I had given up all hope of ever seeing her again.

Looking back, I had no idea how Grandma Long was suffering not knowing where I was or if I was dead or alive. Now this seems like one of the cruelest things to do to a mom and grandma. Why was it done?

It's amazing how good intentions take a twist. No one plans to confuse truth with heresy or do irrational things. But it happens when a persuasive leader uses his position and power to alter the lives of trusting followers.

My Dad's childhood experiences with caring Amish students created a longing for the simple, community life-style they experienced. Even the opportunity to get his degree in engineering at Miles Laboratory expense was not enough to deter him from leaving northern Indiana for the sanctuary of this Amish-type group in Tennessee.

In Indiana it seemed Dad could do anything. He provided food, clothing, and shelter for his family. People hired him to do odd jobs around their homes. He could sell almost anything. He did mason work, laid block and brick making fireplaces, chimneys, and foundations. He built our garage and was in the process of building our new home when he received permission to enter Lael Colony. He was totally committed to the hope for a better life and sold out to move to Tennessee.

During our second fall in Tennessee he left with many colony members to pick cotton in Mississippi. He returned to Tennessee alone several weeks earlier than the rest of the group. He was different, no longer his real self. The dad I had known was gone, and in his place was a man who babbled to himself and did other strange, abnormal things. What happened in Mississippi was a mystery. No one offered an explanation or any information. It was obvious Dad was the victim of a nervous break down.

After about ten years of living in the Lael Colony environment and Mom's excommunication, Dad eventually truly crashed. One day suffering from amnesia he walked off. The county police picked him up, but it took four officers to subdue him and get him into their vehicle. They kept him in the jail until it was decided he should be placed in the Mississippi State Mental Hospital. Doctors there diagnosed him as a paranoid schizophrenic, and he underwent electrical shock treatments. These trying times were perplexing for him and his family.

When my folks first started planning to move to the colony, my mom liked the idea of moving near her family. She was willing to sacrifice everything to follow God. She gave up her new home which was in the process of being built. Following The Elder's instructions, she destroyed all worldly things including all personal records. She burned all legal evidence of births, marriage licenses, honorable certificates, and some photos in order to do what The Elder had told her was the Lord's expectations. What deception!

She had some concerns about the lack of medical attention for her children after Fred's injury in our auto accident en route to Lael Valley. She rationalized that doing without medical attention would be better than burning in hell or having her children burn in hell forever. So she gave up all her past to do what The Elder had said was necessary to wholeheartedly follow The Lord.

Evenso, there were many happy days and months during those early years in the colony.

Being with her parents and siblings was a special joy. She was back in the culture of her childhood. Teaching her children the simple chores and skills was meaningful for her. She was submissive to her husband and the demands of the colony expressed by The Elder's extensive list of rules.

But all was not as it appeared. Family struggles paled significantly one Sabbath when The Elder publicly accused her of possessing money which was contrary to his infamous rules. The meeting with The Elder and his chosen committee provided no relief.

The Elder excommunicated her after she refused to confess to his unfounded claims. He doomed her to hell. His deceptive maneuverings took a heavy toll.

"My life might as well have ended there. I felt I was going to hell," Mom said. "What came from The Elder's mouth was as if God spoke. I was doomed, doomed to hell that day."

Fred was eleven months older than I, but we were true friends. I don't recall him ever getting cross with me or I with him. We were co-workers. Together we could conquer most any task we tackled. Some of those were making large piles of wood, splitting and stacking it, plowing and cultivating our garden with the mule, cutting the grass and weeds in our yard with a swing blade, and repairing a roof. The most remarkable job was tearing down and rebuilding our chimney.

Fred was sensitive, creative, intelligent, personable, and good at putting things together. What one of us didn't think of the other did. We could discuss our thoughts and feelings and find solace in having a listening ear even if our situation didn't change. We made unworkable things work, and we were happy with the results. We were adventurous and welcomed challenges.

We feared losing each other. I was anxious especially after his dangerous fall from a tree and from the top of a cotton wagon. His concern for me was evident the time I was bitten by a snake and the time I turned yellow and almost died. I knew Fred cared without him saying it. We could read each other well. We were never allowed to verbally express how we felt. There were no hugs or kisses. No one dared say I love you. We just knew. We weren't even allowed to touch each other.

Because of the father-son conflict, childhood in the colony became increasingly tough for Fred. Around the age of ten or eleven because of the stress, he began biting his fingernails. Soon his eyes began to twitch, and then his face twisted. Dad had been harder on Fred than Joan and me. I never understood why. Fred worked hard doing things that Dad wouldn't do. It seemed Fred could never do enough to please him.

After Mom's excommunication Fred demonstrated more leadership, and out of concern for Dad followed him as he walked away one day. Fred stayed out of sight, hiding in a ditch because of fear of what Dad might do if he knew he was being followed. When Dad was released from the State Mental Hospital, Fred ran away from home.

That almost destroyed my world. I wondered if I would ever see Fred alive. *Would he be found dead like Uncle David?*

Joan, my sister, about twelve months younger than I, stayed home with Mom when Fred and I started school. Sometimes she helped us pick up stones in the garden. Often when we made a big pile, she wanted to tear it down even when Mom gave orders that the stones all stay there.

Looking back, things surely would have been different for us if we had been allowed to physically play or have games, crayons and coloring books, or even if we could have drawn pictures. Such things were strictly forbidden as too worldly, and that would give the Devil a chance to enter our lives. We might be tempted to draw an image in the likeness of God. So drawing trees, birds, and animals was forbidden. Flowers weren't allowed to be drawn, painted, or even planted in the gardens or anywhere around the house. They would be *zierote* (ornamental or decoration). We were allowed to write numbers, ABC'S, and Bible verses. Besides the Bible we had very few books. For that reason we spent a lot of time outside.

I'll never forget the time we were in the hayloft while Mom milked goats. Joan wouldn't jump from the loft, but when she rolled around in the hay, she caught her hair in a roll of barbed wire hanging on the wall. Fred and I went for help. Mom was busy, and Grandpa came to help. He pulled a knife out of his pocket and cut off hair to free her. What he did was really something. We knew a girl's hair was never to be cut. Now she had a big gash cut out of hers.

Joan and I enjoyed watching the birds. One spring we raised a baby sparrow that we found on the ground. As a fledging, we turned it loose, and it lived in our yard. When we came home from the field, this young bird landed on our shoulders, fluttered its wings, and begged for food. We always stuffed it with food for the night. This sparrow remained tame and our friend for a long time.

The first year we went to school in Mississippi was at Uncle Eli Miller's with his wife, Maude, as our temporary teacher. This was Joan's first year in school. Getting her there was a challenge after we moved to the snake den house. First, she had to learn how to circle around a tree to hide from the bull. Second, she had to learn how to scoot across the fallen tree over the bayou. When the water was high, this was a problem because Joan feared heights. She panicked whenever Fred and I tried to help her across the large fallen log.

"I'm afraid, and I'm not going across that log," Joan would announce forcefully. The rushing water was an added alarm.

"It's the only way across, and we have to get to school," I responded.

"Don't look down," Fred explained, all to no avail.

Joan refused to try.

"I've got an idea that will solve the problem," Fred said. "I'll go first. Joan, you sit behind me, and Lois, you sit behind Joan. We can shimmy across together."

In spite of the rule that we were supposed to stay in line according to age, we followed his directions. I gripped Fred's arms just above the elbows and locked Joan between us. Inch by inch we scooted across the 12-foot log. She held on to Fred and he pulled her along while I pushed her as we edged across. This certainly was a chore for Fred and me, and Joan was always scared stiff.

The Elder appointed Joan and me as partners like he had with many other girls in the group. We were not to go alone any place especially after dark. I didn't mind the arrangement, but at times this seemed a problem for Joan.

I had to be careful or she would have dragged me into some unpleasant situations, and I would get in trouble. She and Fred often had scrapes, and then they both wanted me to take their sides. I tried to remain friends with each. At times this was a very hard position to be in because I truly cared about them both. I was the buffer and go between. I didn't like it when they were not nice to the each other. Fred always treated me kindly even if I helped Joan. Joan resented it when I helped Fred.

Mid year we moved to the house under the big oak tree (see front cover) and finished the school year with Maude as our teacher. After Lael Parochial School was set up in an old shotgun house on the cotton plantation, Naomi was our teacher. Our new school sat between Grandpa's house and ours. I felt happy for a fresh start and a new schoolhouse. I liked walking to and from school, even with The Elder's instructions to walk single file oldest to youngest, Fred, Lois (that was me), and Joan, with no stopping on the way allowed.

I never told Mom how Joan spit on me because I couldn't tattle or complain. If I did, I might have been spanked for tattling or complaining, and I wouldn't chance it. Often when one child tattled on another, both received punishment, one for tattling and the other for what they did wrong. That's just the way it was!

I enjoyed watching the birds. We made birdhouses, put them up, and watched the number of eggs laid and hatched by sparrows and starlings. Mom helped us make a martin house. Dad helped us cut a tree down, attach the martin house on top of it, dig a hole in the backyard, and put up the martin house. Then we enjoyed the nesting martins. Their calling other martins in from the sky fascinated us. We made trap doors over the holes in the martin house and attached strings that ran into our kitchen. When a sparrow or starling invaded the martin nest, we pulled the string and entrapped the martin's enemy, thus helping the martins win their battles. Not allowed to kill anything ourselves, we had hungry and willing cats to help solve the problem.

We had a bird book and enjoyed seeing how many different wild birds we could spot. We liked the mockingbird, doves, indigo buntings, and the towhee. The starling is a mean bird, but the shrike was one of the meanest birds we knew. The shrike killed smaller birds and stuck live grasshoppers on barbed wire fences.

We had our laying hens as pets, and they were all named. On the Sabbath we would sit on the floor and let a hen walk onto our lap and sit down, but we could not pick them up because it was the Sabbath. Some hens liked to sit in our lap and have us pet them. On the Sabbath we were allowed to watch the hens lay eggs.

We also had our pigeons all named and enjoyed watching them nest. Dewy and Queenie, our first pair of pigeons, came from a pole barn on the plantation. The plantation manager gave Dad permission to get two baby pigeons out of a nest. Fred climbed up, got the babies, and brought them home. We enjoyed raising them and then watching them raise young. This provided meat for us.

We liked pigeons with white on them and always dreamed of having one that was all white. One day a pure, white pigeon came to our barn; it acted lost and stayed in the area. I made a trap door with a string on it running into our living room and trapped this special, white pigeon. This seemed too good to be true. We had plans to give it a mate and were excited about it having babies. Then one day Dad demanded, "You catch that white pigeon. I'm giving it away because you give it too much attention. That makes it an idol."

This dampened our spirits. It seemed so unfair, and it crushed me. My heart cried after all the hard work I did climbing my ladder, setting up a trap door, and hooking up a string just to catch this special, white pigeon. It was the one we had so longed for, and it seemed God had sent it to us. Now it was gone forever! No more white pigeons ever came again. This painful lesson taught us not to give anything much attention or show or tell our feelings. I was ready to get the onions out to peel and slice or dice because that was the only time we could cry or have tears. I always wondered *why we can't cry because the shortest verse in the Bible says, 'Jesus wept.' So why can't we cry without onions?*

A stray tiger cat that we called the Mother Cat chose to live at our home. Then she had kittens. This cat and kittens were the first ones we had to enjoy since our Indiana days. Some of our cats made good raters and mousers especially Runt, Springy, and Baby. Other special cats were Squally, Mitzy and Ringy. They made good heaters in bed on cold nights and made us miserable in the summer. They brought fleas into our beds, and flea infestation became a problem. Our cats multiplied to 22, all interbred with some sick and diseased. Eventually we were forced to keep the cats out of the house because of diarrhea. We were not allowed to medicate or destroy any cats. The cats staying outside helped our flea problem inside, but the mouse problem increased in our home.

To stay warm at night in the winter we heated bricks on the wood stove, and then rolled the hot brick up in an old rag or rug and took it to bed. The hot brick did not keep those gray, beady-eyed, little mice from running over me and across my bed at night. I recall one night I brought a cat in to catch the gray critters. This excited the cat and caused diarrhea to shoot from under it's tail messing up my bedding. It was a big job to wash all the bedding so we resorted to our home-made mousetraps.

The rule about fighting was broken when Joan and Fred had their spats. I didn't like to see any of their confrontations. Joan liked pinching contests which I refused to participate in with her or Fred because it seemed hurtful. It hurt and she always got mad. Fred took her on at times, and she would get so angry. We also participated in the contests of seeing how long we could hold our breath. I seldom won and didn't really care because it gave me a headache. Fred was usually the winner.

On the Sabbath our family often had contests to see who could find the books in the Bible the fastest. We also had contests for finding chapters and verses. This seemed fun. We also had contests and drills on saying the chapter headings for every chapter in the Bible. We drilled on the nine-blocks of scripture The Elder gave us to memorize, some full chapters and some several verses. This kept us sharp on Bible memorization. We were to learn a Bible verse a day. I had a lot of verses stored in my mind.

Mom made Joan her helper setting the table, making food, and washing dishes. Joan was unhappy with that arrangement. When spring came, she wanted to feed the chickens and pigeons. Mom would give in and so Joan and I traded chores. Joan often didn't finish barn chores in time for breakfast, and she got tired of them and when it got cool or rainy, she decided she wanted the kitchen job back. Mom would give in rather than listen to all of Joan's dissatisfactions and let her help in the kitchen again. I had to do the outside barn chores. *Why?* Mom once tried having us take turns and that didn't work either. When Joan helped in the kitchen and was told to help pump water or do some of Fred's chores, they would spat — secretly.

One time we all felt very sorry for our rooster. He was cocky at times but much more so when men entered the chicken house. The rooster could see the men's feet move, which seemed to upset him more; the ladies long dresses covered their feet. Dad heard this rooster would attack people so he went into the hen house set to teach it a lesson.

The rooster attacked him. Dad broad-handed him across the side of the head. The rooster returned ready to fight. Dad hit him harder on the side of the head flipping the poor thing head over toes and spinning into the air. The rooster landed wrong and severely broke his leg. He could not walk for a long time. We spent a lot of time splinting his leg with a couple of sticks and white tape. The other chickens pecked him so we penned him separately. It took a long time for his leg to heal, and it was crooked the rest of his life. When we finally butchered him and he went on the dinner table, it was easy to see how bad the break was. Some of us couldn't eat a bite; that rooster was a special friend. The bone had a lot of calcium built up and was over lapped at the break. I never wanted this to happen again and never told Dad if a rooster threatened us.

A joy our family shared came to our house as two baby puppies. We named the puppies Shag and Shortie. They were brothers yet so different — Shortie shorthaired, short legged, and sassy, Shag longhaired, taller, and quiet. We enjoyed them both until Shortie was killed on the road.

That was another sad day for our family, but there were more to come.

Chapter 3

A Family Left Behind

The Colony — forced to move from their once paradise land — departed on orders from The Elder. Hopes for peace and a better life burned in hearts and minds as we moved from the rocky Tennessee valley to a fertile, flat, cotton plantation on the Mississippi Delta near the levees along the east side of the Mississippi River.

We did not create a caravan and travel together to our new home. Each family packed and moved only when directed to do so by The Elder, one family at a time.

The Eli Miller family was the first to leave Lael Valley in Iron City, Tennessee, for the flatlands of Coahoma County, west of Dublin and south of Clarksdale, Mississippi. It had been known as the Gurney Plantation and Allen Williams was the manager.

It was the fall of 1954, and my family was the next to be ordered to move to Mississippi. Upon our arrival we lived with Uncle Eli's family of six, making a total of eleven in the household. They shared with us the last room in the back end of their shotgun house.

Off the main gravel road, two long, winding, dirt tracks with Bermuda grass in between wound through a cow pasture and led to the house hidden in the middle of a large cotton field. It was surrounded by a wall of trees. The Millers lived in three rooms in the front, and at the back of their house we had one room for our bedroom and an enclosed back porch that we used for our kitchen. The outhouse sat in the backyard.

Our homemade beds had three levels. My bed was the

one in the middle. Fred slept on the bunk above; Joan had the bunk below. Once I awakened in the stillness of the night, I heard a strange noise that lasted only a few minutes. It resembled the sound of a hoot owl. Wide-awake and half scared, I listened intently until the sound stopped. Then I dozed off again. In the morning, I told Mom what I heard. She had heard the racket and told me that the scary sound was Uncle Eli while asleep was sing-songing an old slow German hymn from his childhood.

This was the first and last time I ever heard a human sing in our colony. His singing sounded more like moaning and whining to me. Although I never understood a word, it captured my curiosity. The only kind of singing I knew about were wild birds, such as the mocking bird and the many others that lived in our former Tennessee valley home. Singing for our people was strictly against The Elder's rules for he considered it as a sinful way of the world.

Why, I wondered. *We read in the Bible that people sang. Were they worldly people? Maybe they were worldly or Gentiles! But what about King David singing in Psalms?* I didn't understand why, but I accepted our rules whether they were about singing, eating, or work.

I liked sharing a house with Uncle Eli's family and their orange cat, Tiger, and their dog, Tan. With their four children around, all older than my brother, sister, and I, much more action filled our lives. With the two boys and two girls in their family and the three of us there was always somebody doing something.

I learned about peanut butter from them, and I liked it. One time my dad gave me a big heaping spoonful of peanut butter and told me to take it all at once and swallow it all. I did, and I felt like I nearly choked to death. He found it fascinating, but he did finally give me a drink of water. I never knew why he did that, but I learned a tough lesson.

That fall at the age of six picking cotton proved to be adventurous, challenging, and a very hard, tiring task for my first year of fieldwork. We rode to and from the fields in the back of Uncle Eli's pick up truck with his family. Boys sat on one side and girls on the other. We picked from daylight to dark every day except Saturday, our Sabbath, and the days it rained. The plantation manager paid each father a penny a pound for the cotton his family picked. It took 100 bolls of cotton to make a pound. I tried hard to make my hands roll quickly from one fluffy, white, cotton boll to the next, and then scrambled through the cotton stalks to pick as much cotton as I could so Dad received enough pay so that we had food.

Each person pulled a long cotton sack with an opening at the mouth. Each sack had a shoulder strap so it could be pulled along as we picked cotton as fast as we could to feed our hungry sacks, and to make them fat and full. We smaller children were given the shorter seven-and-a-half-foot long sack our first year, and the adults used nine-foot sacks.

Near the end of cotton picking season rain came and water stood in the clay furrows between each row. We walked in deep mud and waded water to gather the cotton crop. In these wet areas we used short homemade sacks about three feet long and sixteen inches wide, tarred on both sides of the bottom and with a short strap on top which hung from our shoulders. We called them our mud sacks. They kept the harvested cotton dry, held about twenty pounds, and we weighed and emptied them often. The cold wind blew and dried the cotton bolls making them much lighter. Consequently it took more to make a pound of cotton.

After twelve-hour days working in the field, we children were worn to a sleeping frazzle and often unable to stay awake to eat supper. Our evening ritual began with our floor prayer, The Lord's prayer. At the table Dad read aloud one chapter from the Bible, and he ended the ritual with a table prayer. He always said the same prayers which had been given to him by The Elder. After prayers it was time to eat. Dad kept us awake for the Bible reading, but when we shut our eyes for the last prayer, sleepiness overpowered hunger. Nevertheless we had to stay at the table until everybody was done eating even if we went to sleep and never ate.

After completing the cotton picking season our first

winter in Mississippi, Mrs. Eli Miller, Aunt Maude, taught school in the front room of their home. Meanwhile, Naomi Miller taught the children who were still living in Tennessee.

Early that winter my parents asked The Elder for permission to move into a house east of the Amazon field. It was a mile southeast of Uncle Eli's if we went through a cotton field, the woods, across a bayou, and a cow pasture. We waited and waited till early March when finally The Elder gave approval for us to move.

We had to walk a mile to Uncle Eli's for school. Down the dirt field-road leading to and from our home, through a cotton field, under barbed wire fences, and across a cow pasture we went. Often running we dodged fresh cow paddies so we would not stink like manure. We dashed behind trees or climbed them when the mean Black Angus bull chased us. Often with hearts pounding, we circled behind trees to escape from the snorting, pawing creature with his head lowered to the ground until he tired or wondered off with the cows. Then we ran as fast as our legs could take us.

We trudged through the woods and usually jumped across the water in the bayou. When the water rose high, the large fallen tree served as our bridge. We shimmed on our bottoms or bellies across the log, using our hands to pull and our feet to push. Sometimes there was six to eight feet of rapidly, rushing, muddy water a few inches beneath our toes. After passing through the rest of the woods and another cotton field, we arrived at school often dirty from circling or climbing a tree, a fall in the mud or manure, or a jump across the water. Arriving at school clean proved to be a rarity because we usually had cold, wet feet, and sticky, muddy boots.

Our first family home we called the snake den house because in the side yard was an old cellar half caved in and full of trash where rats and snakes lived. This became more entertaining than our hen house of pullets. Standing atop the side cellar wall we spent hours on the Sabbath quietly watching rats play, and we saw their fear of snakes. We witnessed one rat captured, bitten, and its life squeezed out of it as the snake coiled around the poor critter before slowly swallowing it whole.

We were fascinated by one snake with babies. Surprise the snakes with a quick move, and the babies popped in their mother's mouth quicker than the blink of an eye. Later they all came back out. Snakes and rats were everywhere it seemed. There were more rats here in Mississippi than in Tennessee valley but fewer bad, poisonous snakes. Thankful to have our own house we worked hard to clean the bare wood floors and walls, nail tin over rat holes, and fix broken and airy windows.

One day as Dad worked on the roof, he found lodged between the roof and chimney a perfectly smooth, egg shaped, chocolate colored, rock-like object that was precious. I still have it today and have taken it to a specialist who said it might be a meteorite which did not burn up.

Meanwhile, my Uncle David Miller, who had been in hiding three years in Tennessee because of the draft laws, came to Mississippi before his family. He stayed in the back room we had lived in at Uncle Eli's. After school my brother, sister, and I were allowed to visit him a few minutes each day. He seemed to enjoy us, and I became attached to him. He encouraged us to be good and do our best in school. We helped him catch *mooka* (flies) in his windows and put them outside to go free since we were not allowed to kill anything according to The Elder and the Bible in Exodus 20:13, *Thou shalt not kill.*

The spring of 1955 we worked chopping cotton. We did this the first time we worked through each field at the beginning of each growing season. The new rows of two-leaf, baby cotton stalks looked like a thick, green, twine rope about an inch thick strung atop the dark, soil ridges which ran from one end of the field to the other. This chopping the stalks caused better growth. We chopped out a hoe-width gape of the tender, young cotton leaving six inches to the next standing stalks. We learned to chop cotton fast and accurately, leaving no less than one and no more than five cotton stalks in each hill. We had to get all the weeds in the process and often that meant bending over and pulling weeds around the young cotton stalks. After that first time through, the fields were hoed to keep the weeds and grass out until picking season started. For hoeing and chopping cotton, fathers received for pay one dollar and fifty cents a day for the small children, and for the older children and adults three dollars a day. Everybody worked from six o'clock in the morning until six o'clock in the evening.

One day we chopped cotton in a field across the bayou and through the woods south of our house. In that field were lots of tough, red vines which dulled the hoes. The file for sharpening them was left laying on the front porch, forgotten after sharpening hoes that morning.

"Lois," Mom called to me, "you're fast and dependable. Run home as fast as you can and get the file laying on the front porch. Hurry back so Dad can sharpen our hoes at our noon break."

"Sure!" I answered and swiftly ran toward home. I ran into the woods, up the bayou bank, down the bank to the bottom of the bayou and made a long jump across the stream of water. I hustled back up the bank and down the other side sprinting at full speed until the big toe on my right foot tangled around a hardened bamboo stump. With a machete knife, Dad had chopped a path through the bamboo thicket leaving many ten-inch high, sharp, bamboo stumps sticking up out of the earth at an angle. When my toe contacted the bamboo stump, my body went into a spin. I sailed through the air landing face down flat on the ground. I soon felt pain and warm blood flowing. *I must hurry on,* I thought. I tried to get up, but pain took me down. I tried to crawl; pain and blood stopped me. I began to feel faint and sick.

What am I going to do? I'm supposed to hurry! I sat on the ground tightly holding the arch of my foot to stop the blood flow. When I let go, blood gushed. Gripping my foot tighter and without a sound or tear, I lay on my side rolled up in a ball. Minutes turned to seasons! Enough time had passed that I should have the file back to the field. Then Mom came over the hill with a look of disbelief.

A Family Left Behind

"What happened?" she asked.

"Mom, I stubbed my toe and it's bleeding."

"Let me see it." One look and Mom whispered, "I feel weak too. I see the bone inside your toe. I'll go back to the field and get Dad."

My family returned and Dad carried me home. Mom insisted on washing out the gash that went three quarters of the way around my toe and down to the bone on the inside toward the other toe. She bandaged my big toe to the one beside it and wrapped the front part of my foot with rags from worn out clothes. Dad and my brother and sister went back to the field with the file and hoed that afternoon. Mom stayed home with me. The next morning my toe and foot had swollen extensively. Nevertheless I went to the field and sat at the end of the rows with the water jug all day. I learned to hop on one foot.

A few days passed and infection settled in my toe and it smelled like something dead. Mom had me soak my toe in salt water every morning and evening. By the end of second day of soaking, I had learned to walk on my heel. Then we put a good wrap over my foot and a piece of plastic over that, and I hoed cotton. It took weeks for my toe to heal and for me to walk on it normally. The scar remains today.

Later we moved from the snake den house to an old four-room, shotgun house dwarfed under a huge, round shaped, oak tree and located on the gravel road east of Uncle Eli's. This was the house where I spent most of my childhood.

In 1956, The Elder released Grandma and Grandpa Miller's family to move from Tennessee to Mississippi before cotton-picking season began. At first for a short time they lived in a vacant house at the end of the Pump House field. During that time Aunt Polly Miller, age twelve, became terribly sick with extreme stomach pain. It was believed she might have appendicitis. She screamed and cried out in pain. Her family tried to convince her not to scream. They even tried to cover her mouth with a pillow. Nothing worked in the fall, hot heat! So they closed the doors and covered the windows with comforters to block the sounds from any plantation worker who might be passing. We feared Polly would die. Miraculously she lived. After several weeks of recovery she returned to normal.

Grandpa's family then moved to a house east of us and on the same gravel road. Uncle David moved from Uncle Eli's and lived with his family. It was not long before The Elder came to Mississippi and stayed with Uncle Eli's family. He lived in the room Uncle David and my family had once lived in.

Sabbath meetings were held from one o'clock to four o'clock at Uncle Eli's house until a shotgun house between our house and Grandpa's was clean and repaired for our schoolhouse and worship. It seemed the colony was joining together again. This felt good. We went to Grandma and Grandpa Millers to eat, visit, and help in the garden. We also enjoyed picking wild blackberries together along the woods when the cotton was too wet to pick.

In the fall the group picked cotton from daylight to dark and weighed every sack. We knew for Dad to get a penny we had to work hard and fast for the weight to add up. When the cotton was dry and light, it took more than one hundred bolls to make a pound, and when it was green or wet it might take a bit less.

Lael Parochial School and all the schoolbooks from Tennessee were moved into the old shotgun house between our house and Grandpa's house. One room in the shotgun house served as our school for many years. That's where I attended class until I was forced to leave the colony. The Elder ordered a small room to be made for him inside the back room, using about half the space. Naomi Miller taught school that fall in Mississippi, and I learned a lot that year.

Meanwhile tension was growing. The Christian Amstutz family remained the last members awaiting instructions to vacate the Tennessee valley. They became deserted and forgotten by The Elder. Oppression and depression invaded this family. Susanna Amstutz, one of the abandoned there, informed me years later about how and why they left the valley.

A Family Left Behind

Unable to make a decision without The Elder's supreme approval, Christian could not understand his abandonment. Neither did he comprehend why The Elder ordered the departing families to build a fence across Swanagan Branch Road, post a no trespassing sign, and pile rocks up at the gate between his allotted four hundred acres on the south end of Lael Valley and the rest of the deserted colony. Susanna later described it this way, "I felt like we were being stoned to death. For more than two years we were left forsaken in the valley in Tennessee. We were totally isolated from the colony. Even worse we had lost communications with The Elder."

Christian, not knowing what he had done to be cut off, never strayed from his belief that The Elder was a 'Man of God.' He was sure that if there was any error, it was within himself. Few people have endured more for their choice of beliefs than did Christian and his fellow believers. They were very faithful and did not want to be like the complaining Israelites.

Christian's children had no school during that two-year period. His son, Luke, was emotionally and physically incapacitated because of his leg injury. He did not know what was happening with his oldest son, Joseph, whom he had hauled off and dumped on the east coast as The Elder had commanded. One of his younger daughters, April, became physically handicapped and speech impaired. His oldest daughter, Mary, whom The Elder instructed the family to use a *mieding* (shunning) on had walked out of the valley after two years of torturous shunning. She found help from outsiders, the Roy Robertsons, and left the area.

The Amstutz family did not plant much of a garden believing The Elder would tell them to vacate the land. Their cow had not freshened for some time and they sold her. Their food supplies diminished. Salt, sugar, and flour were down to nothing at times and so was money to buy it. For something sweet, they tapped the maple trees and made syrup.

After two years and in great distress Christian went outside the valley a good distance and found a farm job.

Later two of his sons went with him and worked there too. He admitted to lying awake at night and listening to the whippoorwills and hoping God would give him a message through them. He also watched for sunbeams and asked God for signs from them. Finally having enough money for gas, he drove to the Mississippi Delta, went to my grandpa, Benjamin Miller, and Christian said, "*Ick shpeah givilich on ick vill vissa fon De Elder vos fa du fa de velli gaya.*" (I feel clinched up and want to know from The Elder what to do as far as leaving the valley.)

Grandpa went to The Elder and told him, "Christian is here and wants to know what to do about leaving the Tennessee valley."

Refusing to speak to Christian, The Elder responded, "Tell him, 'go east to escape hell. Get out of the valley now and fast.'"

Grandpa went back and delivered the words to Christian.

In fear, Christian hurried back to Lael Valley and put out a fleece to see if God would give him a sign. Sure enough one Saturday morning the message came to him. They were to get out of the valley quickly. He told his family that Sabbath, "Flee the valley for your lives. Go to escape hell. We must be out before sundown if we are to survive."

They locked their house and opened the hen house door so the chickens could get out to water in the creek and find food. They had no knowledge when or if they would return. Their dog, Shep, followed as the family fled as fast as they could with only the clothes on their backs. They walked in single file according to The Elder's orders. Father was first, then the boys by age, and then mother and the girls by age. When they came to the east gate and fences, Christian instructed his family to go under the barbed wire fence as The Elder always did, to lay on the ground horizontal with the fence and roll under it. One by one they lay on the ground and rolled under the fence and out of the valley.

Christian was greatly relieved to be out and grateful God had spared him and his family. They walked to the top of the first hill and waited until the Sabbath was over at sundown. Then they walked to the Roy Robertsons for help and stayed there until Sunday morning. They then went back to the hilltop just outside Lael Valley's east gate and camped there for more than a week.

Christian and the three older children went back into the valley, got their truck, and brought their belongings out. They sold most of what they brought out. They kept only necessities such as clothes, sewing machine, cooking utensils, and mattresses. Once his wife, eight children, and dog were positioned on his truck he loaded on what he could without an inch of space left. The rest of their belongings stayed on the hilltop including some mattresses and their old black iron kettle. No furniture or extras of any kind went along. Christian drove his cramped up family east on a long hard trip.

Christian connected with his mother's sister, Lydia, and her husband, Eli Chupp, who were Old Order Amish in rural Dover, Delaware. The Chupps were in the shunning with Christian and also were previously with his deceased parents and did not welcome them to stay at their house that Friday morning. He sought a quiet place before sundown to spend the Sabbath and found only the community dump where they settled in that autumn evening. They anticipated staying until Sunday morning, but when their truck refused to start, their departure was postponed. The dump seemed quiet even after a light snow, and Christian became less motivated to find a better place.

In a few days he located the Richardson produce farm in Camden, Delaware, where he went to work. For two months he returned to the dump to eat and sleep with his family. Then two of his boys found work with him and later the girls did too. They worked under contract packing apples. Susanna recalls embarrassing moments saying, "We were the spectacles of the community."

Christian was informed that the welfare department was planning to take his school age children. He wrote to them saying he could not allow his children to go to a public school because it would displease the God of the Hebrews whom he served.

In spite of shunning, the Chupp's sympathy for the Amstutz family did allow them to park in their yard at night. Christian and his three boys slept in their hayloft, and the six ladies slept three to a mattress in a small shed. Because they had left the dump, the welfare department and school officials left them alone.

When space was available, the Amstutz family moved to a labor camp for migrant workers. The long buildings were made of concrete blocks and had cement floors. They had no running water in the buildings. To start with the Amstutz family lived in two small rooms and later in five rooms. Each room had an outside entrance like a motel. While living at the migrant camp, they picked cucumbers and asparagus, extremely backbreaking jobs.

After leaving the camp Christian rented a two-bedroom house for his large family. Later he rented a larger seven-bedroom house with an inside toilet which he still didn't allow his family to use. They made and used their own outhouse, and they pumped water by hand from a pitcher pump as The Elder had taught them. When not busy at the Richardson farm, they picked peppers for the Amish and were paid by the basketful. They also picked potatoes, cauliflower, and peaches for neighboring farmers.

Meanwhile The Elder lived in Mississippi with most of the remaining colony. He stayed busy with writing, giving orders on setting up the meeting places, the school, and giving more rules as well as instructions to print his Scripture Line and El-Elohe-Israel books.

The Tennessee paradise land was now totally deserted by all the colony members and left to the wild life. The houses, barns, sheds, and schoolhouse were left to rot. Two families sold their portions of the land, and to some The Elder said, "Never sell that land. God gave it to us and to God it shall return."

That is why some of the land remained vacant over forty years until September, 1998. An heir decided to sell my grandpa's three hundred acres, the last land left of the colony's over two thousand acres.

Before the auction day I stood on grandpa's land awestruck as memories flashed in my mind. There were many good times as a small, innocent child in this once paradise place. There were thoughts of Uncle David, and how free, yet, hidden and happy I thought he was there. Yet I wondered, *why all the pain, agony and confusion? Why did some suffer and hurt on this beautiful piece of isolated earth?*

Why must this property be dissolved?

Wasn't this our Promised Land?

Patricia Hochstetler

Chapter 4

Death Brings Authorities

That gloomy, humid, fall morning a full-blown emergency occurred when one of the most secret persons in the colony was missing. Uncle David, who had been in hiding for over three years, went for his early morning walk as usual before daylight. He never returned.

At daybreak that Sunday morning, Grandpa frenzied that his oldest son was missing. Instead of going to the field he went to The Elder and said, "David went on his morning walk before daylight and never returned. He's missing! I want to go looking for him. Is that okay?" Grandpa pleaded.

"Don't go looking for David! Don't call the law. Don't report anything to the plantation manager or owner. And don't say a word to anybody outside the colony. Trust God to work things out according to His will," The Elder declared.

That tough day seemed never ending as we went to the field and tried to pick cotton. Our thoughts swirled with astonishment. Mentally we were bogged down. Emotions, which dare not show on our faces, overwhelmed us. By evening, the sun had set and still not a trace of David! Days two, three, and four passed. Still no David! Concern consumed us. The air was filled with silence. Every person's thoughts were etched with fear. Forced to go on to the field as usual, we worked hard and trusted God to take care of David and everything.

My heart was deeply saddened to think Uncle David was gone. *Where could he be? Will we ever visit him and catch* mooka *together again?* I believed we would.

On Thursday, the fifth day of his absence, we all went

to work in the cotton field. Mid-morning a sheriff's car drove up to the end of the field. Two officers walked down the cotton rows toward us. Complying with The Elder's previous orders about dealing with outsiders, heads stayed down, faces were expressionless, eyes focused on all the snowy cotton bolls, shaky hands rushed for the next bolls as fast as possible, knees shook, and hearts trembled.

Grandpa stopped and looked up as the officers approached him. He waited for them to speak. The officers disrupted our once tranquil colony as they lurked near by, questioning and scrutinizing every move.

"What's your name?" the sheriff asked Grandpa. "Who are all these people? Who are you working for?"

Grandpa was silent and everyone waited.

The sheriff continued, "Last evening two boys were squirrel hunting three miles away and found a dead man who resembles your people. Do any of you know who the man could be?"

There was a long awkward pause!

Grandpa couldn't handle the pain. "My oldest son, David, has been missing for five days," he whispered.

"Why didn't you report a missing person then?" the officer demanded gruffly.

"We hoped he would return," Grandpa sheepishly replied.

"How old is your missing boy?" the other officer growled.

"David's twenty-one," Grandpa answered.

"Then why doesn't the plantation manager know of him if he is from your family and working for him?" the sheriff asked.

"David was studying the Bible to become a prophet like our leader. He didn't work in the fields, and he had been depressed for days," Grandpa soberly told the officers. He did not reveal that his son, on orders from The Elder, was in hiding to avoid registering for the draft.

"It appears somebody shot this man. The death looks suspicious, and you aren't being too cooperative," the officer threatened sternly. "We *will* find the killer."

The officers began questioning all the fathers in the colony and Zack, David's seventeen-year-old brother. Of course, Zack, like all the colony children, was instructed not to answer any questions from the public. To every question the officers asked he replied, "Ask my father."

The officers then spoke in rougher tones to Zack, and in obedience to The Elder's orders he still did not answer their questions. He stood with footprints frozen in place, lips sealed, and trapped in his mind and body. The officers sharply snapped more questions at him.

"Boy, if you don't answer our questions we'll shoot your legs off," an officer shouted as his hand was in position to draw his gun. Shaking in utter fear, Zack answered them the best he could with his limited English skills. The rest of the colony, as scared as a group of rabbits with hound dogs on their trail, watched and listened for the next move. After questioning, the officers left everybody working in the field except for Grandpa, Dad, and Zack who they ordered to go to jail for more questioning.

After leaving the field the officers stopped at our schoolhouse to question The Elder who greeted them saying, "Greetings in the name of Christ Jesus, the Lord whom *I* serve."

"Come on, you're going to jail for further questioning," the officer said, getting little response. The officers put The Elder in the squad car and slammed the door. They also stopped at Grandpa's home and questioned Grandma and Naomi, David's oldest sister.

The sheriff then chose to take Naomi and Grandpa to the funeral home to identify the body. It was David's.

Detectives at the jail questioned each one separately and then released Dad and Zack that same day. They kept Grandpa and The Elder in jail overnight for further questioning.

When Dad and Zack were released from jail that Thursday afternoon, they began digging David's grave in a nearby, small, country cemetery. David's two younger brothers, Enoch and Besodiah, also helped. According to Dad his fury raged inside and with nearly each shovel of dirt he thrust out of the grave he repeated, "This should have never happened."

The officials released Grandpa and The Elder after extensive questioning. "The jury selected will determine if there was any foul play that caused David's death," the officials announced. Grandpa and The Elder refused to eat any jail food, so neither of them had eaten or had clean clothes. Grandpa, taken from the cotton fields, dirty, frail, and now despondent, looked pathetic.

Comments made by the public suggested that our colony had made a human sacrifice. We knew there was no truth to the accusation, but we felt trapped by the situation.

To determine the cause of David's death the coroner immediately selected a jury. They originally decided David met his death at the hand of another person or persons and that his open wound was caused by a large caliber bullet. At one point we were led to believe that David was possibly stabbed with a knife, leaving his large wound. The investigation continued a few days, and the jury left its verdict open pending completion of the research and autopsy.

Before sundown on Friday David's swollen body was placed in a homemade wooden box, quietly slipped into the freshly dug grave, and quickly covered with earth to prevent more flies congregating and the stench from filling the air. No services, viewing, or further ado was made.

Only memories of David remained like a relentless wind rising and falling and beating on our minds. The sun set that evening and our Sabbath began quietly. No outward emotions. Only inside mourning. I heart-cried all day without a tear. I ached inside. *Why did Uncle David have to die this way? Why? Why didn't The Elder order us to put on sackcloth and ashes as the Bible said to do while mourning?* I wondered. *Did he mourn?*

The colony remained scared of the police, the law, the government, and *de velt leit* (the world people). With *moot los* (low moods) we waited with a shadow of great fear of the worldly people coming after the other young men in our colony.

The appointed jury later met in the cow pasture where David's body had been discovered under a large oak tree. They found where David placed his straw hat, Bible, flashlight, and money belt on the ground by the fence. They saw signs indicating David had climbed over the fence to climb the tree. Small branches and leaves had been removed from the tree where his body came down. The deputy sheriff and the coroner concluded David fell or jumped about seventy feet to his death.

The autopsy failed to reveal any foreign object in David's body. The physician reported that the broken bone and wound could have been caused by a torsion fall with the leg twisted at the moment of impact. This sent the broken upper portion of the leg bone gashing outward causing the wound first thought to be made by a large caliber bullet or a knife. The report stated that shock and exposure probably caused death. Authorities believed David met his death accidentally with suicide mentioned as a possibility.

Word came a few weeks later that the jury declared there was no indication of foul play in David's death. This gave the colony people much relief.

Grandma confidentially told Mom, and years later Mom related to me, what had happened with David. In distress David went to The Elder a number of times in the past year to deal with the natural phenomenon of wet dreams. Each time The Elder said, "This makes you unclean. Take a bath before sundown. After sundown that evening you will be clean again according to Leviticus 15:7. Keep trying and it should not happen again." Such deception!

David was depressed because his problem continued to occur. He expressed that he should be able to control himself even while asleep and it was his fault. Once again the night before David walked away he went to The Elder for advice. Encouraging him again to keep trying, The Elder counseled, "Fight off fleshly things and go for spiritual things."

Having more courage and confidence the next day that

it would not happen again, David went to bed that night in good spirits. Four-thirty in the morning he woke when he heard his mother up. He got up despondent and told her, "I feel too unclean, evil, and sinful to be with the family any more." David walked away troubled.

Grandma knew the wet dreams had happened two consecutive nights, but she never considered that David would not return from his walk. He was not to be seen in daylight hours because of his draft evasion.

For three and a half years David stayed hidden inside the house by day and outside only in the darkest of night and then only on dirt-field roads, in woods, or bushes. If full moon was out bright, he did not go. As a young child, I did not fully know of his pain in confinement nor realize how pale he looked from no sun. I knew he desired to be free and outside in the sun during the day, but he could not. My thoughts went to the joy of visiting with Uncle David after school and catching *mooka* in his room, the time he rescued me from hanging in a tree, how he helped Mom pick corn, and helped Dad cut timber. His death was shocking. *Why did it happen?* I wanted to know.

As a young child, David's death was the first human death I had to deal with and the first in the colony. For years I wondered what actually happened to him once he left his home early that Sunday morning. *How did he feel? What did he think? How many days did he live in the woods before he met death? What did he do before he died that October day in 1956? Where is he now?*

If I had seen a trace of him dead, a service, a funeral, a burial site, his grave after burial, a grave marker, or anything, maybe it would have seemed more real to me. I saw nothing. I knew it was true he died because of what I heard. Yet I had dreams he was found and I talked to him. That felt good, and I wished so much it would happen.

I was told this was something God allowed to happen, maybe to test our faith. We didn't have to know why, but we should go on, forget it, and try to please God so it will not happen to more of us. I did not understand all I knew and heard, and it seemed impossible to forget David and all that had happened in 1956.

In 1996 I spoke with Willard and Hazel Williams, the property owners of the land across the road from where David's body was found. Willard answered my many unanswered questions. "I personally saw David Tuesday at noon," he said, "and a lady in the area told me she saw him about two in the afternoon. He looked white as paper and was very thin and walked slowly and appeared weak like an old man. He walked down into the bayou, came up on the highway, and walked past our house. I didn't recognize him or I would've gone out and said somethin' to him. He later walked back going the opposite direction and went back into the 'bou' (bayou) and walked toward the direction his body was found the next day."

Willard expressed that likely David's life ended shortly after he saw him walking because of the appearance of his body. Lying in the fall heat caused rapid bloating. Willard knew the boys who found David. He walked to the death scene when the authorities arrived.

The things Willard said he witnessed helped me to conclude that David spent about three agonizing days alive and hungry from early Sunday morning to at least Tuesday afternoon. I also concluded that David was looking for help or he would have never gone on the public highway or walked in front of houses with the chance of being seen. These actions were totally unlike him. I know he had to be desperate and wanting help. After going where people could see him and still not finding help, I'm sure he felt it was impossible to find any way out of his situation.

In 1996 I also interviewed the undertaker who handled David's case, and he indicated that David's open wound appeared to be from the broken upper leg bone which had stabbed through the bowels and came out the lower stomach area. I asked if he felt David lay and suffered very long, and he didn't believe he did because one would likely bleed to death fairly quickly after an injury like that.

Tragically David's life ended at the edge of the woods

in the cow pasture protected only by the umbrella-like large oak tree. Desperate and alone with feelings of unworthiness to stay with his family, he chose a lonely final walk in public view.

Colony members — still stressed and struggling to deal with David's death — received tragic news. Willie Miller, an excommunicated member, was arrested, immediately placed in the county jail, and finally went to trial. He was sentenced to serve two years in prison for draft evasion. This raised even greater concern for all the young men still in our colony and generated fear of the government closing our school.

The Elder seemed upset with the colony members. He would chide us, "You are not doing good enough. You're in the 'red' and not doing well. You must do better. Keep your lips sealed and follow the rules," The Elder warned.

Then The Elder announced, "Fathers are to do all the communicating between me and their families. Colony members are not to be visiting and talking back and forth between families any more. I'm placing a separation between families."

This hurt so badly I could hardly stand it. We had no more meals at Grandma and Grandpa's. Each family was to keep to themselves, be on their own, and not depend on each other. In school we could only talk about class work with each other. Talking even that limited amount was better than nothing. It was really sad that parents and children no longer went to each other's homes. In obedience to The Elder, only fathers carried messages to each other and The Elder.

"Eli Miller family, you and I will leave the colony and this cotton plantation. We will become nomads in the land and nobody will know where we are," The Elder announced one day. "For a while you will become squatters stopping to work wherever you find it before moving on."

The Elder and Uncle Eli disappeared, and the rest of the colony had no idea where they went. It seemed unfair that Uncle Eli had broken his agreement with the plantation manager to work for that cotton season and without saying anything. The plantation manager found out Uncle Eli's family of six had deserted, but nobody revealed that The Elder had ordered this and gone with them. It remained a huge secret where they were. The perplexed people strove desperately to serve God and get back in the good graces with Him. We prayed for The Elder's return and for direction and guidance to get back on the right track. Grandpa especially seemed upset with The Elder's disappearance and blamed himself.

Early one morning before daylight, the eastern sky lit up. Grandpa's house had caught fire! Dad rushed out and ran there to help. Because of the family separation that The Elder had earlier placed on the families, Mom and us children could only sit on our front porch praying that they would all be alive. We watched billows of fire rolling upward.

Black smoke towered high above flickering sparks and flames. Flames shot hundreds of feet into the morning sky and lapped up Grandma's and Grandpa's home. Scorching heat penetrated our faces as low-tone voices echoed in the distance.

Reflections flickered on us as though a giant candle lit the dawning skies. *Did they all survive? Is Dad okay?* We wondered and waited with anticipation and many questions for daylight and information of what actually happened.

My grandparents' house burned to the ground in minutes. Our colony accepted no help from the public or outside world. Fire remained smoldering in a big tree in their front yard after daylight while their house, belongings, and many memories lay on the ground in a huge heap of red-hot ashes. We were too far out in the country from Clarksdale where the nearest help existed. No fire trucks or any help would have been allowed to come on the property had they shown up. Their help would have been unwelcomed on orders by The Elder.

Dad finally came home and said, "A sparrow's nest beside the chimney started the fire when they lit the first fire in their wood burning stove. The dry, ancient, slave house ignited like a box of matches. They lost much of their belongings, but thankfully there was no lost of life."

Grandpa's family lived in the schoolhouse temporarily. The family expressed feelings that their home burning was a sign of God's wrath on them. The plantation manager moved the snake den house that my family once lived in to Grandpa's yard to replace their former dwelling. We continued praying for The Elder to return and to help by telling us what to do after this tragic warning of a fiery hell.

Suddenly one day Eli Miller's family showed up with a message. At first we felt delighted to see the lost family. However their message that The Elder had a nervous breakdown was another blow. They claimed The Elder had gone crazy and walked the streets shouting and claiming he had killed a man. The police arrested him and put him in jail. After some time passed authorities could not find evidence that The Elder had killed anyone and they released him.

The colony refused to believe the Eli Miller family and their claims about The Elder's nervous break down. The colony reasoned that the Eli Miller family accusations were false and that they were *hoch gonga* (gone high or astray.)

Years later I interviewed Uncle Eli's family. They had nomadic ways and traveled around as Gypsies for some time before they finally settled in Laurel, Mississippi. That's where The Elder, while living in their home, scared them to the point that they abandoned him, leaving him alone in their home. That's when The Elder went on the streets and went crazy.

On my investigation tour in 1996 I interviewed a neighbor who witnessed the police arresting The Elder on the bridge as he shouted at young people who were swimming near the bridge. The Elder was still shouting when the police arrested him and hauled him off.

How can we live without our leader?

Chapter 5

A Day of Reckoning

Rain had forced us out of the field and left the ground too soaked to return. No nine year old would complain because they couldn't hoe cotton all day. So after it quit raining I went to Grandpa's house. Aunt Kay and I were sent to deliver a meal to The Elder. He had a Jewish cook book and ordered a dinner based on one of the recipes. It consisted of corn beef hash with steam-fried cabbage and onions, sprinkled with plenty of salt and pepper. We also took fresh home made bread and butter, a banana, and fresh water. We headed out across my grandparent's blossoming garden to the schoolhouse.

I chased butterflies along our path and enjoyed the sounds of the singing birds. I was enjoying two special blessings: we were out of the field, and I had the privilege of going along to deliver a meal to the prophet of God. Once at The Elder's chambers I watched as Aunt Kay set out the meal. It was fine until The Elder turned to me and said, "Lois, you have been a good girl today. Keep up those good works."

His words upset me. I had not seen The Elder since the last Sabbath meeting. *How did he know if I had been good or bad? If God talked to him as he claimed, God would not lie. How can this be? God and I know the truth of what happened today.* My mind did a couple back flips to a few hours earlier that morning at daybreak, but I never said a word about it.

When Aunt Kay and I left The Elder's place, I was not chasing butterflies on the return home. I wasn't talking much either. I couldn't share my thoughts with anyone. No! Not a soul on earth dared to know my thoughts, and I knew it.

Why? Well, if I mentioned what I did, I would be in trouble. If I mentioned it after The Elder said I was a good girl today, I would be calling him and God a liar, or I would be declared a liar. This was too much trouble for me to handle. I couldn't tell anyone what I did.

To make matters even worse Aunt Kay commented, "I'm glad you try so hard to do right. The Elder even knew how good you have been today. That's great! I encourage you to continue being good and doing your best every day."

This gouged into my opened, wounded conscience. I had always wanted to do right and be good. But early that morning in the field I had to go to the toilet, and the woods or bushes were the only place to go. I hurried off to the bushes with my hoe in one hand and picked green leaves for my toilet paper with the other hand. In the bushes deep enough to be out of sight, I quickly dug a hole with my hoe as The Elder had instructed everyone to do when using the earth as a toilet. I relieved myself, and then using the hoe covered my relief as a cat does.

Meanwhile a group of red winged black birds hovered over my head in disarray as they scolded me for invading their nesting area. Then one swooped down and nearly struck my head as I began to walk away. There before me in plain sight was the bird's nest in a low bush. I peeked in. Four beautiful, greenish blue, rust-speckled eggs lay in the neatly lined and finely woven nest. My parents — knowing my fascination with birds and their nests — strictly told me not to touch any bird's nests, their babies, or their eggs.

Temptation consumed me! *Were the eggs warm or cold? How did they feel? How heavy were they? How many more specks were on the under side of them?* I wanted to know, feel, and see more, so I picked up one egg and examined it. It was warm, smooth, lightweight, with the same amount of specks on the under side. As I went to put the tiny egg back in the nest, it slipped out of my fingers and fell to the ground. There lay a bloody, tiny, baby bird kicking and gasping for breath without any hope of a future life. I felt terrible. I had disobeyed my parents and the Bible and killed a baby bird. I helplessly watched the undeveloped bird turn cold and give up on life. Words cannot describe the empty ache I felt inside. Guilt raged within. The sobering reality of what I had done registered as the day continued. I caused the birds to lose one of their children. I felt sorry for them and knew they had reason to scold me.

I knew God watched me every second and saw every move I made. He knew what I had done, and He wrote it all in my heavenly record. I asked God to forgive me, but I didn't feel forgiven. *I will have to answer for this on judgment day I know. Well, I won't say a word to anybody and only God and I will know my secret sin of disobedience.* That decision didn't help. I still felt convicted, guilty, and ashamed of my sin. I was truly sorry and hurt, but I could not go back and undo what I had chosen to do because I was curious. I would have to suffer the consequences of my action, endure my guilt, and hope nobody found out.

Now why did The Elder say I was a good girl that day? This was a huge mystery to me because I was far from good that day. Yes, maybe all thirty days prior to today I had been good, but today I was disobedient and guilt radiated off me in waves. *How can The Elder be the man of God he claims to be — whom God talks to — and say this to me?*

I didn't sleep much that night while wrestling with this problem. I settled on what I had heard many times before. I concluded I am too carnal to understand spiritual things. *Could it be a test of my faith? Should I tell Mom or somebody before they find out?* This bothered me.

The next day it rained all day. Mom went to visit her mother and I went along. Aunt Kay told Mom what The Elder said about me yesterday, and Mom reaffirmed how good I was. This scratched into my sin wound deeper. Aunt Kay asked me to go with her again to take The Elder his dinner. I could not say no, so I went with this thought. *The Elder said I was good yesterday, what will he say to me today? Because I have really been good, very good, and done nothing wrong that I know of. He might say I have been almost perfect today.* On our way to deliver the dinner this time we discussed the garden vegetables and canning them.

When we reached the school house and knocked on the door to his private room, The Elder took one look at me and said, "Lois, today you are not doing so well. You haven't been as good a girl today as yesterday. You need to do better and improve."

I melted inside like butter on a one hundred-degree hot Mississippi day. Disbelief and defeat that this could actually be happening to me overwhelmed me. *What would he think next time if I ever came to his house again.* I never did and I never wanted to because I felt wedged into a tough corner and judged by the Almighty. Yet something felt wrong. I became satisfied to think this was a test of faith and that I could not and would not ever understand this situation.

After this incident I felt guilty and struggled with The Elder's words. On the second night I got on my knees and sincerely asked God to forgive me for all my sins. I promised God I would never again knowingly disobey Him or my parents. This day of reckoning was a life-changing event. After that I worked very hard every day to keep that promise and commitment to God and learn His word.

A couple of weeks passed and The Elder without knowing my thoughts or commitment wrote a prayer for me personally and sent it home with my Dad. He instructed that this was a kneeling floor prayer for bed time and should be said according to Matthew 6:6 and said in a secret closet. The prayer The Elder gave me is this:

"I pray and give thanks to Thee LORD, for Thy kindness to me in the name of JESUS.

"I pray for guidance that I may learn how I should behave before Thee and that I may know to do those things that are pleasing in Thy sight.

"Forgive me my trespasses as I forgive others, and allow me to see the way of Thy righteousness which can keep me from the evil. For I desire some day to praise and honor Thee with an upright heart so I may be found worthy by Thee to receive a place within the bounds of Thy kingdom. Amen."

I quickly learned this prayer and faithfully said it every

night before I went to bed. I did this while kneeling and bowing down on the floor in our walk-in closet that was used for sponge baths and praying.

I hoped for a better tomorrow.

Patricia Hochstetler

Chapter 6

Hoeing Cotton

Depending on the spring rains, hoeing cotton usually began in early April and lasted till about August. We worked Sunday through Friday from 6 am till 6 pm and were paid three dollars a day. Saturday, our Sabbath, was our only day off.

We worked on the Gurney Plantation on the Mississippi Delta located in southern Coahoma County. This was east of the Mississippi and Big Sunflower Rivers, south of Clarksdale and west of Dublin and Tutwiler.

At first and because I was so young, my dad was paid only one dollar fifty cents a day for my hoeing. They considered I could only do half the work of an adult. Some days I was allowed to rest in the afternoons especially when I had a toothache. But once I turned seven I was expected to work a full six to six shift and keep up with the adults. Then Dad was paid three dollars a day for me working as an adult. Toothaches or not I had to keep working unless it became so bad it was impossible.

Our usual day began with Mom waking us between 4:30 and 5:00 am so we could get our chores done before breakfast. Mom set her wind up alarm clock for 3:30 or 4. She rose early to start a fire in the kitchen, wood burning stove. She made breakfast of eggs and grits with drop biscuits and sometimes pancakes or leftover fried mush with hot thick molasses syrup. Oven toast was a treat. If we had bread that needed to be used before it spoiled, we might get toast or bread pudding. Mom also made sandwiches every morning for our packed lunches to eat in the field.

My chores took me out in the fresh air and woke me up for the day. It would have been nice to stay inside where it was warm and dry, but I enjoyed my outside chores in the early morning. Sometimes I had to use a lantern or flashlight as I ran through dewy grass or rain. Often at daybreak I was greeted by eager and happy singing hens. I felt cheerful and happy.

I started my chores by feeding and watering the chickens and pigeons. Then I helped Fred with his chores, filing hoes and pumping a keg of drinking water to take to the field. We had a place on the side of the truck where we anchored the water keg. A place under the homemade camper seats held all our hoes. Joan was appointed Mom's helper in the kitchen.

Dad often lay in bed until the last minute while we waited for him. As soon as he got up, our first ritual was a floor prayer where everybody bowed down on the floor with knees, elbows, and folded hands on the floor, head bowed down on hands, and face toward the floor. We lined up across the kitchen floor, and our heads were pointed north when we bowed down. For our floor prayer, Dad repeated the Lord's prayer as instructed by The Elder. We quietly listened to Dad say these verses from Matthew 6:9-13. *"Our Father which art in heaven, Hallowed be thy name. Thy kingdom come. Thy will be done in earth, as it is in heaven. Give us this day our daily bread. And forgive us our debts, as we forgive our debtors. And lead us not into temptation, but deliver us from evil: For thine is the kingdom, and the power, and the glory, forever. Amen."*

Once that prayer was said we went to our permanently assigned places at the table. Dad sat at the head of the table with Mom on the front bench. Fred sat at the opposite end of the table from Dad. I sat in the corner on the back bench, and Joan sat on my left near Dad. When we were settled in place, Dad read aloud one chapter in the Bible as we quietly followed along, each in their own Bible.

The Bible reading took several minutes depending on the length of the chapter Dad read. We were ordered to start at Genesis one and read through to Revelation twenty-one. Only a few chapters like Psalm 119 and a couple other long chapters were split. The Bible reading usually took more time than eating. I enjoyed it in the morning when I felt rested unless he was reading a genealogy in the Kings or somewhere. I often wondered how many times we read through the Bible at the table all those years. After the reading was over Dad said a table prayer given to him by The Elder.

Then Mom pulled breakfast from the oven, the skillet, or whatever kept it warm on the stove top. Everybody was to remain quiet, keep elbows off the table, and eat. Once done eating we excused ourselves and drank the hard, orange, iron water. We used the one floating, long-handled, granite dipper in the white, granite, water bucket which sat on the end of the board, kitchen counter top. We had no drinks at the table. The only milk we had after we left Lael Valley was canned or powered milk. We didn't care to drink that milk from a glass like we did when we had the fresh cow's milk. So we drank the orange, iron-filled, Delta water, and it took a long time to get used to it. The only juice we ever had was tomato juice.

After our breakfast Shag, our dog, was given leftovers, and what he didn't eat the cats ate. When our food was scarce, Mom made Shag and the cats a pan of cooked cornmeal for breakfast. If we had enough time, we washed and dried dishes; if not, they sat till we returned home in the evening. Our dishwater was always heated on the stove, and when we were through with it, we carried it outside and dumped it on the garden.

We often left for the field with great tension knowing that if we were late getting to the field, we had to stay after 6 pm to make up the time. Because Dad and Joan hated to get up promptly it caused stress for the rest of the family. They often left for the fields looking like an unmade bed; yet we worked all day. I made sure I had myself ready and my chores all done, and then I helped others. I seldom felt the morning pressure because I could do nothing to change the way things went, and I realized I was not responsible for

Dad and all that went on in the kitchen. I tried to stay out of the way of the angry ones and be happy and helpful to all I could. I enjoyed helping Fred sharpen hoes and pump water if needed.

My dad was the only person The Elder gave permission to drive the truck, but all the men drove the other farm equipment. Dad made a camper for the back of the 1948, black, pickup truck, and we piled in there to go to the cotton field. He sped down the gravel and dirt roads leaving a tornado funnel of dust swirling behind us. There were few stop signs on any of those country and field roads, and the county gravel roads had no names. Dad still had his Indiana driver's license. Whenever it rained, we dashed home from the field. Carefree, we would see who could spot the most dogs, cats, or a certain type of bird on our way home.

When we reached the assigned field for the day or week, each person took their special marked and fitted, sharp hoe. We made sure we had a good hoe scraper in our pocket to clean caked dirt off our hoe. I also made sure I had a new Bible verse in my pocket. I memorized it as I worked, and it was hidden in my heart by the end of the day. We found our assigned rows according to our ordered line up and began hoeing as fast as possible. It was fun to try keeping up with our aunts, uncles, and cousins. We often marked places to race to or aimed for the end of the rows. This made our days interesting.

When we reached the end of our rows, we all helped our family members finish before starting a new set of rows. Then we worked extra hard to get to the other end where the water was on the truck. Sometimes we could not keep up with Grandpa's family and would pass them in mid-field going in opposite directions. We often hoed long areas in Dad's row to help him keep up. But it seemed we always had to help him at the end of the rows too. There were many things that could cause one to fall behind — extra thick Bermuda grass patches to hoe, red vines, big cockleburs, tall Johnson grass, or the long distance walk to reach woods or bushes for a call of nature.

Hoeing Cotton

We always avoided being seen whenever possible, but there was a greater emphasis on total silence with strangers and only limited conversation among colony members. In the spring it always felt scary when the cotton stalks were small and we could not hide in them. Neither could we take a few steps and hide behind the house or barn as we did at home when working in the garden and a truck went down the road.

Our first time through the fields in the spring was called chopping the cotton. The mounded rows laced side by side were covered with long, green, ribbon-like stands of cotton stalks with two leaves. They stretched from one end of the field to the other.

This first time through the young cotton we thinned the stalks by chopping out a hoe-width of cotton stalks. Each six-inch chop had to be accurate leaving one to five cotton stalks to each hill. Some did not like chopping cotton, but I enjoyed the challenge of being able to chop accurately and maintain a good speed. I found a rhythm as I walked and chopped that worked well for me. I could hoe right or left handed and it made no difference which side of the row I worked on which helped when passing others. Many did not like to race chopping cotton, but I enjoyed it.

When the cotton plants were small, there was also a challenge to see what we could find in the fields like ancient Indian arrowheads and some old coins or old marbles. I seemed to spot them well and enjoyed keeping an eye open for them. Of course, we weren't allowed to keep any coins - not even pennies we found — because The Elder made it understood that only fathers were to have any money. We gave Dad all the coins, but we could keep arrowheads. Marbles were a gray area that we could not enjoy or play with. I believe some were thrown away and some put away. They were considered *veltlich schmucha spiel stoff* (a worldly ornament, play stuff).

Each spring when hoeing started, the women and girls soon suffered sunburned faces. Our skin peeled several times before we could tolerate the hot Delta sun. The Elder banned the women from wearing any hats. That was considered wearing men's clothing, a serious offence. The men all wore straw hats in the field.

The women all had floor-length dresses, slips, and underpants. They also wore long sleeved blouses and tight homemade bras. All these layers worked as insulation for heat and cold. In the heat our layers became soaked with sweat. We were covered well so nothing but our face and hands would get sunburned. Men were ordered to wear long handled underwear, union suits, and long sleeved shirts and heavy denim pants. This is how we dressed year around.

Some days were extremely hot and some of us had signs of heat strokes. It took a while to get over them. When the cotton was young, we couldn't hide our bodies in the shade of the stalks to help stay cool. We wiped sweat from our brows with our long sleeves which left the upper inside dirt brown. If the wind blew, we faced it to cool off.

Once Fred strapped a thermometer to his back and the mercury climbed to 120 degrees. Temperatures like that usually with high humidity became nearly unbearable and we had to drink a lot of water those days. We never had any ice to cool food or water. When heat threatened us too much, we hung a wet towel or handkerchief around our neck until it cooled off, usually by late afternoon.

We watched the clouds and waited and begged them to pour rain so we could have a break and cool off. Watching the weather was a big attraction for us. We knew of many cloud types but not by their common names. If it rained us out of the field and the garden was too wet to work in, we often pumped a 55-gallon barrel of wash water, put lye in it to soak over night, and washed clothes the next morning. Then Mom didn't have to take a half-day off on Monday to wash our clothes. We only had about three sets of clothes. Our best set was always for the Sabbath.

We kept an eye on the *navi sonn* (side suns or sun dogs), rainbows, and rings around the sun and moon. We guessed whether it would rain or not. On dewy mornings as the cotton stalks grew taller, we became soaked to the skin and dried off by mid afternoon. Later we made plastic skirts and tops to shield us from dew and wore *iva shoo* (over shoe or boots) till the dew dried. Sometimes those extra things made it hotter, and then we would be wet from sweat. With all the moisture, blowing dust and dirt we worked in, our bodies often appeared chocolate-covered by the end of the day.

The second time we hoed a field it was to restrain the grass and weed growth caused by the warm, Delta spring rains, and sunshine. It was also a time to thin any extra cotton stalks left in each hill. The cotton would be six to twelve inches high by this time, tall enough to cast enough shade to walk in and cool the soles of my bare feet.

I learned a snake had the same idea when it bit my foot. Fred was ahead of me as he and I were racing to reach the end of the row. He turned when he heard my gasp of pain. "What's wrong?" he asked.

"A snake bit me!" I squealed as I fell to the ground. Then I grabbed my foot and was fearfully silent.

"Are you going to die?" Fred yelled as he rushed back to me.

"I don't know. I might." We looked at the fang marks on my foot.

Fear was evident on his face. "I've got my pocket knife. I can make an x and get the poison out?"

I didn't answer, and instead we quickly twisted my long dress tail around my leg to keep the venom from circulating up my leg. We watched closely to see if it was swelling. It was one of the scariest things that happened to me while hoeing cotton. Since we did not go to doctors, we continued to wonder if I would die. But God spared my life once again. I felt grateful and wondered, *why does God keep giving me second chances in life*. The two long, scratch-like, fang marks on my foot healed without any further problems.

Before the cotton stalks began getting squares which covered the flower buds, the manager had the cotton sprayed with DDT which sometimes made us sick. They sprayed the fields for cotton bollweevils. When we saw the spray rigs coming down our rows, we stepped aside and yielded the right of way to them. After they passed we stepped back and continued hoeing among the cotton stalks that were now wet with a dangerous chemical.

The cotton flowers were pretty. The buds opened to a soft, creamy yellow flower in the morning and closed up at night. The next morning it reopened with a soft, yellowish pink color. The following morning it was a deep, reddish pink. The fourth day it had turned brown before falling off and leaving a tiny boll. Honeybees liked the cotton flowers, and we had to be careful not to touch them and get stung. Sweat bees also stung us when they sat on us and we accidentally touched them.

Other flowers I admired were the maypop, delicate flowers also called the passion flower. I liked the morning glory flowers and had to hoe them out of the cotton no matter how pretty. I often wished I could transplant them to the woods, but we were not to plant or like flowers because they were to *zierote*, (ornamental or decorations) and a liking of the worldly people and we were to be different from them.

We usually took 30 minutes for a lunch break and went under a shade tree to eat our peanut butter sandwiches or biscuits with tomato, lettuce, sliced onions, or breakfast leftovers. And we rested! Sometimes we ate in the shade of the truck or under the wagon if the woods were too far away. During hoeing season there was not much to snack on at the end of the fields until the wild berries and the maypops ripened. I really enjoyed the taste of both and when we found them, we had a short feast. When the wheat ripened, we chewed a handful until it became wheat gum. This was a favorite and our gum treat until the wheat was harvested. Then we waited till next year's crop. We also chewed honeycomb wax for gum and sometimes paraffin wax that we put on canned jams.

Once Dad received full pay for us to work all day there were plenty of warnings about spending too much time eating or looking for food at the edge of the woods. When the cotton stalks were small we had to go to the woods for a toilet rather than to hide in the cotton field. We had strict instructions from The Elder how to use a hoe to dig a hole like a cat does, go in it, and cover it up once done. Green or dry leaves, sticks, or corncobs served as toilet paper in the fields and woods.

Around the time hoeing started we had the Trespass, a Jewish observance, which gave us a week off. The plantation manager was informed of our observance days and understood we would not work at those times. We were also off work to commemorate the Day of Atonement. For that occasion we fasted from all food and water all day, sundown to sundown. This was a hard day for me. I felt so weak. Often we were too sick to eat after sundown. We would try to drink just a little, and if we kept it down we would eat a small amount of food. The next morning was hard to go on with chores, breakfast, and work 12 hours in the field. Somehow we made it the first day and the second and those to follow were better.

During the hoeing season we went home after 6 pm and worked in the garden so we had food to eat and some to can for the winter. If we had time, we made bread. We cut grass in our yard with a swing blade, and cleaned the chicken roost in the evening. We shelled corn and ground corn meal so we had food for us and for Shag. It was easier to do these chores during hoeing season. We worked from daylight to dark when we picked cotton. I liked the hoeing season the best.

Once it was dark we went to the table. By the time prayers were said and Bible reading was done we were often too tired to eat. Supper was something from the garden, *rivell* soup, pancakes, cornbread or fried mush, and tomato gravy. The only meat we had was on a rainy day when we butchered a chicken or used canned chicken if we had any left. We always went to bed tired out, and it felt so good to sleep even if covered from head to toes with field-dirt and chemical sprays. Although I was tired before going to bed, I never recall failing to go into the closet and say my prayer that The Elder gave me.

Friday evening was always a rush to get everything done

before sundown. We all took a bath that night whether we needed it or not. Then we were clean for the Sabbath. Before my bath I fed and watered the chickens and pigeons, filled all our oil lamps with kerosene, cleaned the globes with an old rag, and trimmed all the wicks. Then I took my bath, and we ate before the sun set. The rush was worth it for a peaceful quiet evening and a day of rest. We could sleep till noon if we wanted on Sabbath morning. Dad usually did, but I couldn't sleep that long.

We were able to get more rest during the hoeing season. We didn't work as hard and the hoes were not nearly as heavy as pulling cotton sacks. But by the end of hoeing season the palms of our hands were hardened with calluses, and we were ready for a change even when it meant harder work like picking cotton.

Year after year we followed this same routine. The only things that changed were what happened unexpectedly like the time Mom and I were struck by lightning. I almost died and David and Grandma Miller did die. Supersonic jets were an interruption and scary. The routine was broken when Grandpa's house burned, Mom was excommunicated, Fred ran away, and Dad had a nervous break down. Each year seemed to have some kind of excitement to remember. Some good; some bad!

But the work was never done.

Chapter 7

Struck by Lightning

A few raindrops and an instant explosion! I was struck down by lightning in a flash. My hoe was ripped from my hands. I had no idea how high I flew before coming to my senses lying flat on the ground. I was in the plum-orchard field where the cotton stalks stood about a foot tall. My body tingled all over. My lips were numb, and the left side of my body felt paralyzed.

Mom lay in a ball face down on the ground several feet behind me. Smoke and a burnt odor lingered in the air. I smelled singed hair even though my head covering remained on. My sister, brother, and dad rushed toward us. Mom stood and then came to me asking, "Are you okay?"

"I don't know," I answered. I continued lying on the ground. The family gathered closely. Eventually I added. "I'm numb Mom. I can pinch my left hand, arm, and leg and not feel it. *Ben ick halfa doht?*" (Am I half dead?)

My brother Fred, a weather enthusiast, declared, "I'll mark the row where you were when you took the last chop with your hoe. I'll mark the end of that row so we can come back later and see how close you were to where the lightning struck the ground."

We became rain-soaked as we left the field to go home. Mom and I felt bad the rest of the day.

The next day my left side was still numb. In time feeling returned to my left side and I was able to work, but I seemed to get cold easily and so did Mom. Later whenever thunderstorms arrived, we were more cautious after this incident and we left the fields sooner.

Within the week we stopped at the orchard field and found the place at the end of the row Fred had marked. We walked down the row to the place I had been hoeing when struck down by lightning. Blasted cotton stalks lay dead in a thirty-foot circle. The marked spot where I stood hoeing was about three feet from the edge of the barren and dead circle. It felt eerie to think if I had been three feet to the left I would have been fried and dead like those cotton stalks.

Little did we know then the consequences that would follow this lightning strike. After many years I still have many strange muscle sensations, sensitivities, and reactions that I never had before. I have a spot in my left leg that will pain instantly and severely. When that happens, I flinch and sometimes feel like I could fall. Then it's gone as quickly as it came. My left heel is very sensitive. And I have a spot almost like a tiny hole in the roof of my mouth that will seep blood. I learned that these things could have been from being a lightning strike victim.

I had one more thing to thank God for.

Chapter 8

Picking Cotton

Cotton-picking season started within a few days after cotton-hoeing season was finished. Occasionally we had two weeks between hoeing and picking, and we had school to make up for a short school year. The picking usually started in August and normally ended in November or December. If the weather was rainy, it could last till January which made school start really late.

During cotton-picking season our day began much the same as during the hoeing season except we did all our morning chores in the dark. Mom rose at 4:30 or 5:00 am. She started a fire in the kitchen stove to make breakfast and in the living room if it was cold enough. Dad slept till breakfast was ready. Mom woke us children according to the time it took us to do our chores — Fred and I, and then Joan. Joan helped Mom set the table and wash and dry dishes. Fred's chores every morning were to pump a keg of drinking water for the field, fix any broken weigh-wires on our cotton sacks, and make sure all our empty cotton sacks were in the back of the pick up truck. Our cotton sacks were numbered according to age, men first then women. I had sack number four.

My chores, feeding chickens and pigeons, were about the same as during hoeing season except I had to carry a lantern because it was still dark. Field rats and mice seemed to flood our place in the fall after the wheat, oats, and soybean harvests. Many times in the morning, I helped the cats catch the running rats and mice when I opened the hen house door. This was a sight to behold when the cats stumbled over each other as they chased the rats and mice. We had a lot of cats that started from one stray!

A few especially good raters and mousers were Baby, Springy, and Runt. They quietly waited at the hen house door, and when I opened it, they went airborne to enter. I dashed in and plugged rat holes as cats caught rats jumping up the walls. Baby would catch and bite them and then go for more. Once I recall him standing with two rats in his mouth at the same time. When there were too many rats in the chicken house, the mice were forced to go to the pigeon barn.

One time I entered the barn with the cats and saw a mouse run under my homemade wooden, pigeon feeder. I quickly picked up the feeder so the cat could catch the mouse, but the mouse instantly escaped by running up my long dress. The mouse crawled to the elastic at the top of my underpants. I felt the creepy little varmint's feet, nose, whiskers, and tail at my waist. Apparently it ran up the outside of the leg on my long underpants and was between them and my long slip.

Quickly I grabbed a big handful of my dress at the waist scooping up the mouse in that handful. I formed a pouch that stuck out like an oversize coat hook, and I twisted it so the mouse could not get back on my skin. I didn't care how many holes it bit in my dress, slip, or blouse. I didn't want it to be on my skin or bite me, but I couldn't kill it for the Bible says, "Thou shalt not kill." *How can I get this tiny beast out of my clothes?* I instantly broke into a sweat on this dark, cool morning as I made sure the mouse was in its own small dress pouch on my side. I heard the mouse scratch and saw it move under all those layers. I had the mouse trapped. *How can I get this mouse out without it running farther up my clothes?*

I wanted to take off some of my clothes, but I had a problem. A long sleeved blouse separated my slip and dress. The blouse had to be unbuttoned down the front and both sleeves. I had to unzip one side of my dress to get it off. I didn't have enough room in the dress to slip it over my head with the mouse's pouch on one side. I only had one hand to work with because I was not letting loose of the mouse pouch! *If I did get the dress and blouse off, how would I get the slip off over my head?* It was not possible while keeping the mouse confined to its pouch. I had too many layers on. I had to do all this quickly. If I lingered too long somebody would come looking for me. *What if they found me only half-dressed? I can't chance that. Time is going fast, and I will be called to breakfast soon.*

I quickly knelt on the barn floor, called the cat, and pulled the lantern closer. I struggled to roll my long dress and slip up with one hand and hold tight the twisted mouse pouch with the other. Once to the inside pouch opening, I called the cat and had it smell the spot. The cat had interest. *If I could only make a hole so the cat's paw could reach the mouse! But if I made the hole big enough for the cat, the mouse would escape. Oh, I wish I could get that mouse by the tail and fling it out!*

Time kept ticking by — at least fifteen minutes by now. I wanted the mouse out! Fearing to open the pouch, I carefully probed around and tightened the spot where the mouse was trapped. I peeked in a tiny hole and saw the mouse's hair and closed it quickly. Then I noticed that the mouse seemed inactive. *It was probably playing possum and pretending to be dead and will pop out. Who knows what it will do or where it will go?* I became braver with each moment and began taking risks to get the mouse out as the cat anxiously waited. I peeked in and saw the mouse's tail. I reached in and touched it. It was limp. Slowly and carefully I pulled out the back half of the mouse, and it was limp too. The mouse was dead. The cat quickly ate the mouse.

What do I do now? I guessed the poor little mouse suffocated with all those heavy clothes twisted around it for that long. I didn't mean to kill it. However I felt guilty that the mouse died. *I made the mouse dead and didn't know it. "Thou shalt not kill." Another of the Ten Commandments I broke!*

Sinfulness taunted my thoughts. *What will my punishment be? Will God forgive me? Now I'm unclean for touching something dead. I must tell my family so they won't touch me and be unclean too. I must also take a bath before sunset, and then I will be clean tomorrow. Why wasn't the cat quick enough to catch the mouse first? I know I didn't squeeze the mouse tight enough to kill it. However I murdered a mouse!* "Lord, please forgive me for this mouse murder. I truly did not mean to do it." I regretfully thought that prayer over and over all day.

I went to the kitchen and told my mom what had happened.

"Hurry to the closet with a basin of water and take a bath as fast as you can and put on clean clothes," Mom ordered. "You must take a bath now because we won't be home before sunset."

I hurried with my bath and was done before Dad got up.

"Don't touch Lois today because she touched a dead mouse, and she's unclean," Mom warned everybody as we sat at the table for breakfast.

All day everybody avoided me like I was a poisonous snake. I was thankful when the sun went down and I was clean again. I was never punished for this sinful act, and I asked Mom why. She explained that it was an accident and was not done on purpose, like the mud doll, and it would be different if it was a person. This left me wondering, but I was satisfied to leave well enough alone and not ask any more questions.

On Sunday mornings we took turns pumping water to fill a 55-gallon barrel. We had to add lye and let it set in order to take the iron out of the water so Mom could wash our clothes on Monday, our wash day. Mom usually took a half-day off from field-work to wash clothes unless it rained, and we were rained out of the field. It seemed there was less chance to get the washing done in the evening or on a rainy day during picking season.

Our breakfast was much the same as in hoeing season. Dad seemed harder to get up when it turned cold. In the winter he liked whole-wheat pancakes with eggs, and sometimes we had hot oatmeal on cold mornings. He said the same floor and table prayers and read one chapter in the

Bible. We all sat at the same places around the table and ate much the same food and drank from the same water dipper and bucket after eating.

A big difference from hoeing was that we had to be in the field and ready to pick cotton at daylight, and the days kept getting shorter. It seemed there was still a rush to make it to the field on time. As long as I had my chores done and did my part to help others, I didn't let tardiness be my problem because I was only a worker bee getting transported from hive to the field to work in the yellow and pink cotton flowers. There was not more I could do than stay out of the way, so I wouldn't get pinched by anger or pushed in jail or squeezed under some sort of false accusations. There was no escape but to concentrate on work and learning verses, and I enjoyed that. I put all questions, doubts, and anxiety out of my mind.

Once at the field before Dad stopped the truck we had our cotton sacks in hand. When he stopped, we rolled out of the back door and ran down our rows in high speed. I always wanted to keep up with Grandpa and my aunts and uncles. I wished so much to work with their family, but after David's death The Elder ordered, "From now on each family must work on its own!"

Our normal schedule for picking cotton was from daylight to dark. But some times there was an urgency to get a certain field picked or a particular amount of cotton for a special reason at the cotton gin. I recall several times we picked cotton by moonlight. That was fun, but I was too tired to enjoy it for long. I even recall picking till midnight. We used flashlights to weigh the cotton, and we had lights on the tractor pulling the cotton wagon.

We were paid a penny a pound for the cotton we picked, and it took one hundred cotton bolls to make a pound. Shortly before I left the Delta in 1964, we were paid three cents a pound. This was extremely hard work. Both of my hands flew all day grabbing cotton bolls until both hands were full. Then I transferred one handful to the other, and I quickly shoved the big double handful into my cotton sack with one hand as the other hand continued to pick two or three bolls more. This process continued over and over all day long and week after week filling our sacks and cotton wagons.

We picked cotton using six, nine, and twelve foot cotton sacks pulled by a strap that went over our head and lay on one shoulder, the right or left depending which hand we used to feed cotton into the sack. I used it on either shoulder because I could use either hand to fill the sack. I liked picking cotton. I started with the six-foot sack, and as I grew I went to a nine-foot, and ended up with the twelve-foot sack.

Once one family member had a sack full of cotton we all stopped to weigh our cotton sacks. Dad hung the sacks on the cotton scale hook. In one corner of each sack we placed a green cotton boll and secured it in place with a wire and made a wire loop to hang the sack on the cotton scale hook to be weighed.

Dad carefully weighed each sack, called out the amount, and Mom recorded it in our record book the amount each person picked. The date and amount always remained on record. Fred and I were officially appointed to empty all our family's cotton sacks.

Fred stood on a long, wooden plank 2x10 inch wide that was lying across the top, back edge of the wagon. I stood in the cotton wagon to help him. After weighing each sack Dad threw the shoulder strap attached to the sack up to Fred. He struggled pulling the sack up the back of the wagon as Dad pushed. As quickly as possible, I grabbed the strap and helped Fred pull the sack over the plank. Fred then took hold of the two green cotton bolls wired inside on both back corners of the sack and I kept hold of the strap. I pulled the strap in rhythm to snap the cotton out of the sack as Fred jerked the back end of the sack. This took teamwork, and we made a good working team.

On hot days I had the worst end working down in that wagon standing waist deep in loose, fluffy, white cotton. With all the clothes I wore it made it like a dust-filled roaster in the heat of summer. There was no breeze, only severe sun heat beating down in the walled wagon bed. We should have had the strongest arms and shoulders of any children on earth. That was extremely hard work. Fred and I, for all those years—at least ten, never had a break. We longed for just a moment to relax but never had it. It never worked for Joan to help Fred for trouble flashed when she did. Mom sat in the shade of the wagon to record the weights, and Joan sat there with her.

Fred and I made our work fun on the days we could stand the heat and cold. The other days were survival days. Fred had the worst end on cold days standing up high on that plank in the wind. I recall climbing up on to the old wooden wagon and jumping in the cotton on cold days. For only a moment I lay in the fuzzy, soft, warm cotton and looked up at the beautiful, crystal blue sky and thought *it would be so wonderful to lay here for an hour. This could be a perfect bed.* It never happened. In the wink of an eye Dad had a sack weighed and pushed up for us to empty.

A big shock came when Fred, at about thirteen, lost his balance walking on the top edge of the cotton wagon and fell to the ground knocking the wind out of him. I felt the fall might have killed him. This frightened me and caused me to think, *What if he broke his bones? Since we couldn't see a doctor, he might die.* After gasping for his breath over and over he did recover, and that put an end to us walking the top edge of the cotton wagons. Before it seemed like a challenge to walk on the top of one-inch boards with a 2x4 end every few feet. If we lost our balance, we jumped into fluffy cotton. We never spent much time walking the top except when we went up the tongue end and wanted to be at the back end or when we were waiting on each other to get down. The top edge on those old wooden wagons must have been about twelve feet above the ground.

Picking cotton put more pressure on us than hoeing. We felt the urgency to get all the cotton out of the fields before the weather became too wet and cold. Picking cotton was much harder and heavier work than carrying a hoe and chopping baby cotton or hoeing weeds. We worked hard. Our hands gobbled up every open white cotton boll within reach filling our cotton sacks fast and making them heavy to drag along.

We enjoyed racing from one spot to another point or to the end of the rows. When we started in the morning, we could race with our aunts down the first rows. Aunt Martha would ask, *"Vit do shteik baumvolle ruppa?"* (Do you want to pick cotton fast?)

After the first set of rows we were behind because we had to help Dad keep up. We could talk to Grandpa and our aunts and uncles when we passed them in the middle of the field or wherever. Sometimes we would even meet them at the end of the field and eat lunch together. We all sat on the ground under the wagon or at the edge of the woods and ate and visited. I liked eating with Grandpa's family and picking cotton with them.

We set a marker like a tall cotton stalk, a cotton flower, or weed, or vine top. We sometimes walked ahead and wrapped a quarter of a boll of cotton on the top of a cotton stalk marking a finish line for our race. We never knew who would win because it depended on how thick the cotton was in a particular row or how heavy a sack one had to pull at that moment. If my older aunts had thick cotton and heavy sacks, I could beat them sometimes even though I was younger than they were.

The main thing was to pick fast and keep going to the end of each row even if in small sections. Once down that first row we had to go back another row the same distance to get water and that made us hurry toward the water keg to relieve our dry throats and parched tongues. We could almost hear that water keg calling us. Water was our only reward. On cold mornings Mom often was involved in these races and would suggest setting a marker just a few feet away. Then she added more markers and kept it going saying, "Work hard and fast to warm up." It worked, and she encouraged us to always work hard and meet our goals and to learn our Bible verses for the day.

We were weather watchers and encouraged not to be clock watchers. Of course men were the only ones allowed to carry watches and those were limited to pocket watches. Fred and I had made sundials. As long as I knew which way north was — and I always did, I had no problem knowing about the correct time. I didn't even need a stick in the ground or a circle. I could tell the time by my shadow when the sun shined.

The first cotton picked each season was more green and heavy with moisture yet not as thick in the stalks. By the second picking, two weeks later, the fields looked like white snowballs among green leaves. The cotton was lighter and much thicker. Open cotton bolls hung there waiting to be pulled from the burrs. By the third picking, another few weeks later, cotton leaves had fallen off and the fields looked like fields of snow. The cotton had dried out and was lightweight.

The five prong, dry burrs around the cotton boll shredded our fingers when we were going at high speeds. Often our bleeding fingers were wrapped with white tape so we could continue picking. Gloves slowed us down too much. My hands were often scratched and rough with painful cracked thumbs and fingers with hang nails and worn and broken nails. We had only scissors and pocket knives for trimming our nails. Our hands healed on their own because we were not allowed any hand cream or medication to help them heal. God healed people according to His will.

We worked hard picking cotton, and I don't recall taking snacks to the field — only lunches. I guess we didn't have enough money to buy any extra food. What we had in the garden had to be for lunch or canned for the winter. It seemed the time allotted was only for lunches. However in cotton picking season there was more snack foods available in the woods and fields like the wild persimmon trees at the end of fields and edge of the woods. They were a most welcome treat.

We picked cotton fast to reach the end of our rows to eat those quarter size, ripe, orange, sweet, wild persimmons, and we ate all we could. First, we ate the ripest ones off the ground that the wild animals had left. Then we shook the tree and hoped for more ripe persimmons to fall. With this fruit if we bit into one not ripe enough, we were sure to pucker up and spit it out. The half-ripe, yellowish orange ones made our mouth feel like we had a mouthful of alum. To test if a persimmon was ripe enough, I bit a tiny hole in the skin and lightly touched my tongue on it and could instantly tell without shocking my mouth with a pucker. We could never take much of this food home because we didn't have time to pick any extra or a cool place to keep it, and the ripe fruit would soon spoil. There were also two plum orchards I recall that ripened before the persimmons and those plums were also a tasty treat we cherished.

Another fall favorite was the maypop patches which had the round, yellow, ripe, egg-size balls filled with a sweet, seedy fruit that made a feast for us. In late fall there were wild pecan trees everywhere that dropped nuts. We learned how to crack those by squeezing two together and breaking them in our hands, and we had a wonderful treat. We did gather some wild pecans near our home and kept them through the winter. There were hickory nuts too, but we had a hard time cracking them in the fields. We had some hickory nuts at home, but of course it took a lot of time and a hammer to shell them.

Cotton picking season could get quite hot and miserable. We learned how to stay down low in the cotton stalks in the heat of the day and pick on our knees to stay cooler or if we were tired, sick, or had a toothache. Grandpa and some others strapped on leather knee pads with a soft cushion padding inside. My long padded dress worked well for knee protection. However going on my knees slowed me down and I could not pull my cotton sack along as well, especially once it had thirty-five or more pounds in it. From noon till two o'clock in the afternoon was the hottest time of day. It was also quite dusty in the cotton stalks with us rustling after cotton bolls.

Many mornings the cotton stalks were wet with dew, and we became soaked to the skin and cold unless we wore our plastic shirts and tops to protect us. We still often got wet. Even our head coverings became soaked, especially when the stalks were tall or when we bent over hustling after low cotton bolls. The cotton stalks ranged from two to six feet tall; the average was four feet. Later in the fall once the leaves all fell off the stalks and the cotton dried out, it was easier to pick. The cotton was lighter and it took longer to pick a sack full. Sometimes when we were tired enough, we moved along on our knees.

After that first killing frost sometime in November, the morning sun melted the frost, and by the end of the day the leaves turned black. The smell of dying leaves lingered for several days The cotton stalks would drop all their leaves, and this made picking even easier since we didn't have to fight all the leaves.

After the frost all the green cotton bolls opened up into fist-size, fluffy, cotton bolls and the fields looked like snow. I had seen freezing rain and ice and frost covered fields but not real snow in the cotton fields, and I longed to see it. I had picked cold, frost covered, cotton bolls and walked barefoot on frosty ground many mornings in the fall. We worked in freezing rain as long as the temperature was low enough that the cotton didn't get wet.

Once it turned cold, muddy, and unpleasant, it could be quite miserable picking cotton. We bundled up in layers of coats, jackets, and headscarves and wore boots. After frost in late November the weather often became wet and muddy. I recall using what we called our mud sacks to finish picking. The mud sacks were homemade gunnysack size that we sealed with hot tar about halfway up from the bottom. We used them to pick in mud and standing water. The mud sack held about 20 to 30 pounds of cotton and hung on our shoulders and never touched the ground. We wadded a lot of mud and water some falls and winters to get all the cotton out.

Picking cotton made me more tired than hoeing. Sleepiness overtook me and my appetite left as I struggled to stay awake during Bible reading. After Bible reading we could lay our head on the table and sleep but were not allowed to leave the table until everybody was done eating. Often while the rest ate I became a dirt-covered zombie that drifted off until the rest finished eating. Then I was excused without a bite and too tired to take one. I always remembered to go into the quiet closet, as The Elder instructed, and say my prayer that he gave me after my day of reckoning. I always said my prayer in the closet and then crashed into bed with dirt and all. Several times I recall falling asleep on the closet floor and sleeping there all night.

One time I noticed how dirty my bare feet were from working in the field and thought they were too brown to touch the bed covers, so I let them hang over the edge and slept that way all night. I was simply too tired to go outside to the pump and wash the dirt off. We were required to wash our hands and face before going to the table, but I guess the rest didn't matter. Our clothes and bedding always seemed to boil clean in our three-legged, big, old, black, wash pot.

The next day was much the same, and we worked hard all cotton-picking season. The most cotton I ever picked by myself in one day was 312 pounds. At fourteen I held the record in our family for the child who picked the most cotton in one day. That day was not a cold molasses, slow day for me, and I will never forget it. I felt worn out and I looked similar to a frayed wash rag. My hands were torn and fingers snagged and bleeding from the sharp, pointed cotton burrs. I taped some with white tape and that slowed me down.

My mom and some of her sisters picked 500 pounds of cotton in one day. The colony top cotton picker was my Aunt Martha who picked 600 pounds in one day. A person picking 500 and 600 pounds of cotton in one day was rare in our colony, and I believe unheard of in the public. We were fast, hard working, human cotton pickers. We could not match the real cotton picking machines in volume, but our cotton was much cleaner and freer of chaff and cotton burrs. Many plantation owners were beginning to use picking machines when we left. They still wanted us to pick the cotton because we picked the rows much cleaner. The cotton we picked graded higher and brought a better price at the cotton gin.

It was a relief each season when we picked a cotton field for the last time. Often the young boys followed with a tractor pulling a bush hog and cut the brown, cotton stalks down leaving two-inch stubbles above the ground. This cleared the fields for plowing.

Each year picking cotton was much the same for us other than variations in the weather and some unexpected things that happened like Uncle David's and Grandma's deaths. The Elder left and Grandpa's house burned. Mom was excommunicated. Fred ran away. Dad had a nervous break down. Our one dog was killed on the gravel road in front of our house, and I got sick and almost died.

Once the cotton on the plantation was all picked we started school. I always looked forward to that. Despite walking to school in rain and cold weather, it was wonderful to be inside near a warm stove all day. Umbrellas were not allowed in our colony. They were too worldly and expensive for our group. The weather elements were short-lived as we walked to school compared to working all day in the cotton fields.

Cotton picking was an extended family affair until The Elder said each family should be on their own and not run back and forth to each other's homes unless there was an emergency. This hurt and caused us not to see Grandpa and his family quite as often.

After Mom's excommunication severe pain struck my family in the cotton fields. I was fourteen that summer, and Grandpa's family would not even start at the same end of the field we did when we came to the field in the morning. They walked to the back end of the field with their sacks on their shoulders and started, and when they met us halfway in the field, they ignored us and wouldn't even look at us. They put their heads down in the cotton bushes keeping their eyes on cotton bolls as they franticly grabbed them.

They stayed on the move and never answered us or acknowledged us in any way.

This hurt! How could it be we turned bad so quickly?

Why were we all bad if Mom was the one excommunicated? Is this a spiritual thing and we were too carnal to understand it? We became as nobodies. They ignored us completely, trashed us, and dumped us from their lives all in the name of God and under The Elder's instructions. Such deception! Oh, how this hurt to the bone!

Would things ever get better?

Chapter 9

Rules, Observances, and Traditions

We kept some Jewish observances and some Amish traditions as ordered by The Elder. We were to be different from the worldly Jews, the worldly Amish, and all of the worldly heathen Gentiles. We were to be God's chosen people, a part of His elected 144,000 that would be in heaven. If we obeyed God's laws, we were to be God's elite, perfect people, whether Jewish born or converted Gentiles.

"The worldly Jews have their observance days figured wrong according to the Bible," The Elder proclaimed. "I go by The Bible, the Old and New Testaments, the moon, and what God tells me."

Such deception! The Elder dared to claim his conversation with God (what God tells me) to be equal with the Bible and the moon. Unbelievable!

"We will not keep all Amish traditions the same as the worldly Amish," The Elder announced. "We will keep God's rules as He instructs me. Unlike the Jews we believe that Christ Jesus is the Son of God."

The deliberate deception was evident when The Elder announced that we would observe the Jewish New Year in September one-day after the new moon. We kept it as a Sabbath with all restrictions The Elder had placed on Sabbath observance. We often made our own calendars and marked our holidays on it. I didn't know anything about worldly holidays or how they were observed. The Elder and fathers used the Almanac to tell exact moon phases and sunset times.

Friday evening before our Sabbath, time would be posted by the clock and announced several times before sunset as having only so many minutes while we scurried about finishing our tasks.

Five days before the Passover, also called the Feast of the Unleavened Bread, we ate no meat. This had little affect on us because we seldom had meat with our meals. Chicken and pigeons were the only meats we had after we moved to Mississippi.

Unlike the 'world Jews' we observed The Passover mentioned in Leviticus 23 and Exodus 12 in September instead of in the spring. The Elder set it fourteen days after the new moon. The evening before The Passover and before sunset we always had what The Elder called a bitter herb meal. According to The Elder we were to have potatoes, carrots, and cabbage from our gardens cooked in water without salt or seasoning of any kind. We served his bitter herb meal with only water and unleavened bread made of only white flour and water. Some gagged on this meal and asked if they could fast rather than eat the bitter herbs, and The Elder said, "No!"

The Elder insisted that we observe the Passover for one week. This was like a fall vacation for us. We had to prepare our meals ahead for two days. We ate unleavened bread with regular meals during that week. If the first or last day of Passover fell on Friday or Sunday, we had a double Sabbath. Double Sabbaths were always hard on our animals because we were not allowed to feed, milk, or care for them in any way, even if they became injured or caught in a fence.

The days between the opening and closing of the Passover week we observed as a half-holiday by refraining from labor such as field and garden work, cutting wood, sewing, washing clothes, washing hair, or mopping floors. We did light work like preparing meals, washing dishes, and straightening our beds. This week we woke to our crowing rooster. In daylight we fed our animals. Most of the week was spent resting, studying, and learning the Bible. We rehearsed Scripture Lines and the nine blocks of scriptures that The Elder ordered us to learn. We had races finding books in the Bible and later chapters and verses. At home

Mom called out the book, chapter, or verse and we hunted them.

This most welcome Passover vacation week came in cotton-picking season and we surely enjoyed the break. Sunrises and sunsets drew our eyes each day that week. We had more time to watch every phase and moment by moment moves of the sun and clouds and colors in the sky than when we worked in the field. We could sit and watch our chickens, pigeons, and other animals including the wild birds and critters. I often sat for hours and watched insects.

Ants intrigued me by the hours on this week off. The Elder referred to ants as little people according to the Bible, and he encouraged us to watch them and never destroy ants or their dirt homes.

"Protect the ants," The Elder ordered. "Strive to be more like them. Be poor like the ants and store up food for hard times, and don't plan for earthly processions. Your treasures are in heaven."

I enjoyed watching the perfect bull's eye of a spider web. How can all that weaving string or thread come out of the small creature? Where does he or she store that web? How do they know the distance to leave between webs and to increase the same amount as they weave to the outer edge? Using their hind legs as hands, how can the spider fasten the web with their tail end? It seemed amazing. They made a perfect bull's eye. Then they sat to rest in the middle of the bull's eye until an insect flew into their web. Instantly they awake and like a streak they attack the poor trapped critter wrapping it with their paralyzing web. Then if they are hungry, their dinner begins immediately, and if not, the helpless bug lay bound until it starved or whatever. This fascinated me yet I felt sorry for the bugs.

We also watched honeybees gather nectar and carry it to their hives for honey, their way of storing up food for the winter or hard times.

We took off work December 25th and celebrated it as Christ's birth. Before our noon meal we read the Bible passage about when Jesus was born. We spent the rest of the day studying the Bible. If the 25th fell on our Sabbath, we made festive foods the days before and ate them cold on that day. We still feasted.

On this day we killed a chicken and ate meat, mashed potatoes and gravy, and vegetables for dinner. We made vinegar pies, a favorite desert with a taste much like lemon pie. We could not afford lemons. This was the time of the year The Elder permitted the entire colony to purchase a small bit of hard candy. It was the square, peppermint, red-and-white, striped kind. I recall Dad often banned me from having any because I had so many toothaches. Nevertheless this was a happy day off work.

The word Christmas and gift giving was foreign to me. Later when I went into the world I thought I saw how heathens decorated trees with all kinds of *zierote, veltlich stoff* (ornamental, worldly stuff). It took me a couple of years to figure out the real reason.

In early spring around March we observed the Day of Atonement by fasting from all food and water for twenty-four hours. In Leviticus 23 we read this day was for the atonement of our sins. This day was especially hard for me. Beginning sometime after noon I felt like my belly button touched my backbone, and I started with dry heaves. By the end of the day I was too sick to function.

Like many other children I became so sick after 24 hours of total fasting that it took a couple of days to recover. We would be too sick to eat after sunset, and if we drank water, we vomited. This left us weak for several days and made it difficult to work in the cotton field. At age four and five, as they watched, my parents let me rinse my mouth with water on fasting days. "Only swish the water around in your mouth and be sure you don't swallow any," Mom said. "Be sure you spit it all out."

I obeyed and never recall swallowing any water. The water in my mouth seemed to help a little until late afternoon when I became really sick. After age six I don't recall being allowed any water in my mouth to help me feel better.

Shortly after the Day of Atonement we observed The

Rules, Observances, and Traditions

Feast of Tabernacles as in Leviticus 11. The Feast of Tabernacles lasted one week beginning and ending with a Sabbath. We often had double Sabbaths when it began or ended on Friday or Sunday. This week was a welcome vacation, usually in April, and remained a week for Bible study. We also observed it as a half-holiday by refraining from any hard labor and only doing light work around the house, much the same as The Passover week but with more feasting. The Elder encouraged people to fast voluntarily. We had chicken dinners and spring vegetables already in the garden such as greens, radishes, and lettuce. We made pies from canned blackberries. We made homemade bread instead of drop biscuits. Once I recall making a marble cake from scratch. Swirls of chocolate and vanilla which we seldom could afford were mixed together, and I made an egg white, fluffy frosting.

After the Feast of Tabernacles, we usually refrained from sugar until the day of Pentecost. That meant no dressing on our lettuce because the only dressing we had we made from vinegar, oil, sugar, and canned milk. We used no sugar on cereals like oatmeal, cream of wheat, or in syrup for pancakes. We enjoyed eggs and grits for breakfast. There was a time The Elder also ordered us to refrain from nuts.

For a short time we observed Purim as a feast day to celebrate freedom for the Jews. This was in the spring. Later The Elder cancelled our observance of Purim. I never knew why.

We were to celebrate Jubilee Year every 50 years, and I looked forward to celebrating it in 1990. However by the time Jubilee came I was no longer in the colony. I was celebrating my own deliverance. Those left in the colony celebrated the Jubilee Year with delight.

We also had the year of release, a land rest every seven years. "You must let your land rest every seven years as the Bible says in Leviticus 23," The Elder ordered. "Whenever you started using the land, farm land, or garden, count from there seven years and let your soil rest on the seventh year."

Ours came in 1962. Our gardens all rested for one year

as a land Sabbath. We gave our land to the Lord. I was thirteen when we had it. We had no garden work, harvests, or canning to be done. That's the year Fred and I rebuilt our chimney.

I wondered, *why don't we have animal sacrifices like in the Bible days.* The Elder had banned sacrificing. *What if my parents had a test of faith like Abraham? Would I be the one in Isaac's place or who would? And would any ram, goat, or sacrifice animal appear?* I felt glad we did not have to kill and sacrifice animals.

The Elder stressed never to lie. Some in the Bible died for lying, and he dramatized how all liars will be thrown into the lake of fire, hell. He ordered total honesty and had all the scriptures to back it up. At the age of five I recall The Elder speaking of the two women that both claimed a baby and how one lady lied. To find the real mother Solomon threatened to cut the baby in half and give each woman a half of the baby. The real mother was willing to let the other woman have the baby so her child could live.

I wondered, *why don't we have baptism. John the Baptist baptized Jesus, and why didn't The Elder allow baptism for us?* The Elder said baptism was not necessary for anyone. I never heard why other than he ordered it.

As for Amish traditions, we were to be humble, plain, and simple. The language, Pennsylvania Dutch/German, was the main language used by most of the Lael Colony people. The Elder never learned Pennsylvania Dutch. He claimed he spoke Yiddish and Hebrew, but I never heard him speak any language but English.

Like the Amish we had no electricity. We used oil lamps and lanterns. We had no inside plumbing and used hand pitcher pumps for water. We had outhouses. We were not allowed to have radios, phones, and cameras, or allow our picture to be taken. Television was unknown to me. We wore no jewelry or had decorative things on us or in our houses.

The *meiding* (shunning) was an Amish tradition that Lael Colony used harshly. In the beginning The Elder highly disagreed — even condemned — the *meiding* used in the Old

Amish Church where my mom and grandparents were excommunicated. He said how terrible the *meiding* was toward people. The Elder instructed Grandpa Miller and all the others he took from that Amish church not to use the *meiding* against members in the *bann* by the church.

"Shunning is not honoring your parents like the Bible says," The Elder warned. "You must honor your parents and obey the Bible."

My great grandparents, Moses and Mary Amstutz, were being shunned by the Amish church. The Elder told Grandpa Miller's family not to shun them. Grandpa Miller shook hands and ate at the same table with his father-in-law. His association with him is the reason why my grandpa was excommunicated from the church he grew up in. The shunning issue is what caused most of the people to be excommunicated from their home church.

Families came from the Amish congregation to see the children who had not become members of the Amish church who now lived under The Elder's grip in Hamilton, Mississippi. It was permissible to speak to children under 12 and send messages to their parents who were being shunned. This upset The Elder.

He was now ready for the convenience of *meiding*. How deceitful! He now ordered the very thing for which he had condemned the Amish.

During one visit in Hamilton by the outsiders, Christian Amstutz parked his truck sideways on the road and temporarily blocked them from exiting the premises, giving them a real scare. The Elder was so committed to his new belief that he ordered his followers to slam the door in the face of anyone being shunned. His group continued to use *meidings* in the most severe ways.

Many years later when my great grandparents, Dan and Nancy Miller, were very old they found where their oldest son, my Grandpa Miller, lived with his family. They wanted to see their eldest son one last time before they died.

When his parents drove from Aberdeen to Dublin, Mississippi, and pulled into his driveway, Grandpa Miller walked out to the truck. When he saw who it was, he turned and walked back into his home and slammed his front door so hard it broke. Grandpa Miller had followed the strict instructions from The Elder, and he broke his parents' hearts. This was a clear twisting of Bible teachings and The Elder's own earlier orders to honor their parents! Such deception.

Much of the same traditional Amish food dishes were served except pork and lard that were banned. Our colony avoided everything that was not permitted by the dietary laws in Leviticus 11. Animals had to have a split hoof and chew the cud, meaning no rabbit and squirrel meat. Fish had to have both fins and scales. Poultry had to be free of webbed feet and kept penned so the chickens would not eat or touch anything unclean for human consumption. Unlike the Amish all our food that was purchased had to be kosher showing a circled K or R on the package.

Many of the Amish ways of raising animals were kept, but pigs were not allowed anywhere. Amish work ways were kept like gardening by hand and with horses. We could have horses and wagons. We could not have any small engines such as garden tillers or lawnmowers. However The Elder ordered the colony to purchase a bulldozer to clear land and make it easier on the men and mules. He also gave the colony permission to have one tractor to run the saw mill. Then he gave permission for several fathers to have a truck and obtain driver's licenses. These licenses did not require a social security number in those days. Nobody was to have a social security number. We were exempt under the non-resistant laws for religious purposes.

The men's clothing changed some from the Amish style. Men no longer wore *de latz husa* (the flop pants) with buttons. They wore denim pants and coveralls with zippers. Men wore work shirts made of heavy twill fabrics. The Elder ordered all men to wear long sleeved long johns for underwear in summer and winter. Unlike the Amish, The Elder ordered men and women to always wear long sleeves.

The men's black felt hats and straw hats remained the same style as the Amish. Anytime the men were around The

Elder he ordered them to remove their hats in reverence to him, God's prophet. This was unlike any Amish practice. The men's haircuts were changed to much shorter than the Amish, no long over the ear bowl cuts. Their long beards were kept like the Amish, only banning any kind of trimming on beards or mustaches.

At first, the colony kept the Amish women's homemade dress style. The Elder — contrary to Amish customs — allowed small prints on dresses for a short time until he declared prints on dresses not good and banned all printed fabric that was floral or striped. The Elder could not make up his mind. He became more extreme than the Amish by ordering limited colors in only blues, grays, white, and black. He ordered all clothes for men and women to be plain.

The Elder designed the women's dresses. He ordered them to make the dresses under his instructions and with his approval. Our dresses were made alike in style and all the same color, pilgrim gray, except for one lady in the colony, Naomi Miller. He ordered her dress made black. Our dresses were made much longer, heavier, and different from the Amish.

Our colony floor length dresses in heavy twill, and pilgrim gray jumpers — tube like style — were designed to conceal any shape. Two-inch wide matching straps crossed suspender-like in the back held the dress up. Four flat layers of navy blue fabric, twelve inches wide, surrounded the bottom which served as weights to keep the wind from blowing the skirt. Sewn inside the front of the dress was a six-inch wide panel of the same twill fabric running from the navel to the knees. Attached to that panel were three stays placed horizontally to prevent the wind from blowing the dress in or permitting it to fall in between the legs. Large pleats on each side above the knees gave freedom to walk. Two one-inch, light blue, trim pieces sewn around the bust line of the dress gave the dress a balanced look. A seven-inch zipper on the left side at the bust line allowed a better fit and made it easier to get on and off. The dress had two large pockets on both sides. Because of the weight of the dress, sewn inside was a waist band that helped relieve some weight from the shoulders.

Under the jumper we wore a long-sleeved, white blouse with a collar, button front, and cuffs all trimmed in navy blue ribbon. When not in the field, we often wore knee length aprons. We wore navy blue socks and tennis shoes or went barefoot.

We could wear long stockings in the winter for warmth or anklet socks in the summer because our dresses were long enough to cover our legs. Our under pants were ankle length as well as our slips which had short sleeves.

The women were not allowed to cut their hair in any way as is the Amish tradition. The Elder ordered us to braid our hair differently from the Amish and pin it on top of our heads. We placed our braids where The Elder ordered which helped fill out our head coverings that he designed. We could use hair or bobby pins.

The Elder ordered us to wear heavy gray head coverings to match our dresses and made from the same twill fabric. We women were allowed to wear any color of blue, gray, or black headscarf tied over the top of our head coverings anytime, and on the Sabbath we were all required to wear only white headscarves pinned under our chins giving a shawl look. We were not allowed to wear any black bonnets as the Amish do or bonnets of any kind not even to shade our faces in the hot sun. "You must wear a covering or a headscarf at all times," The Elder said.

The Elder also designed a tight-fitting heavy, gray headband, matching our head coverings and dresses, that fit tightly over the forehead to prevent any frowning and to press free all wrinkles.

"In bed you must wear a night covering in case you want to talk to God at night and you want Him to hear your prayers," The Elder warned.

More rules seemed to be added as time marched on. Later The Elder ordered the people to cover their feet to pray by wearing shoes, socks, or covering their feet with a long dress tail or something.

Rules, Observances, and Traditions

Unlike the Amish, The Elder banned all kissing, even the holy kisses given at church by the Amish. He even banned all hand shaking.

"Shaking hands means one is in agreement with the other person. We cannot be in agreement with anybody in the world, so refuse to shake hands with anybody even in our colony. Thereby you will avoid any questions as to who you agree or disagree with. Put your hands behind your back or in your pockets, and if any stranger approaches, always say, 'I don't shake hands.'"

Years later a member of the colony was asked why he didn't shake hands, and he said because he was taught not to shake hands with anyone. As an adult, he never knew the reason why he couldn't shake hands and neither did I when I lived with the group. We simply obeyed the rules.

Unlike the Amish, men and women and boys and girls were not to touch each other.

"You are not permitted to touch the opposite sex or anybody unclean," The Elder ordered. "Not shaking hands will also avoid contact in this situation."

The women were never allowed to go anyplace alone.

"I order the women to all have a partner to go with them and be accountable to. Never go anyplace alone. It's safer this way," The Elder declared. "I will appoint each of you a partner that you must go with everyplace."

At first the married people were allowed to live as married couples. The Elder had given my parents permission to marry before he allowed them to join the colony. Later The Elder banned all marital relationships. Unlike the Amish tradition, The Elder ordered no copulation for the married people and total celibacy for the rest.

The Elder announced, "You will be unclean if you have any marital relations or any ejaculation. Masturbation is forbidden and also unclean. You are unclean when you menstruate and even any chair you sit on at that time is unclean. If you touch anything dead, you are unclean. When you touch another unclean person, then you are also unclean. Anytime you are unclean, you must take a bath before sundown and you will be clean again after the sun sets. If you touch a dead person or are in a house with a dead person, you must take a bath and are unclean for seven days. Read the scripture in Numbers 19 about uncleanness and follow those rules. If you have any questions, God will give you the answers through me," he said.

Could The Elder really know everything?

Was he really the voice of God?

Chapter 10

Footprints of
the Condemned

A veil of stifling apprehension settled over me that terrible afternoon in 1962. Our family trudged along with twenty-five other colony members toward the weekly Saturday meeting. At 13 and living on a cotton plantation south of Clarksdale, Mississippi, I was not aware that I was a member of a cult. It never occurred to me there was a word that described the strange world I was living in.

We were dissidents from the Amish religion and led by The Elder, our Jewish leader, who seemed to have come out of oblivion to command our lives. The world outside our farming commune was as alien to me as are the gates of Heaven to the flaming portals of Hell.

As surely as the followers of Jim Jones who committed suicide by drinking poison at his command, or the victims of David Koresh who burned in their compound at Waco, I, too, was a member of a cult. Without a doubt I would have drunk to my death, burned inside a building, let anyone kill me, or done whatever our leader instructed. I lingered as one of The Elder's obedient subjects.

A peal of distant thunder incited a startled gasp among the walkers. Lightning and thunder in our Amish thinking implicitly meant warnings from God Almighty. What would we experience today? A foreboding mood crept upon our family as we had prepared to join the procession. The stress of those moments still strikes me now as I write this.

"I feel The Elder is upset with me," my grandfather, Benjamin Miller, his voice trembling had declared earlier.

He said nothing more.

I knew that harnessed beneath the tilted black, felt hat half-covering Grandfather's eyes, seething fear and terrifying thoughts gripped him. His reddish brown beard concealed most of his expressionless 'brick' face, but Grandfather's feelings were none-the-less evident.

Previously, in a very commanding voice, my Dad had announced, "Wife, The Elder has directed fathers to have complete rule over their families. Wives must submit and children obey. I've done everything The Elder delegated to me. Now go to the bedroom, Mary, and tighten your shoulder brace before we go to the meeting. Perhaps next week I might release you if you can stop rounding your shoulders. You know how The Elder wants all our women to walk upright, straight!"

Thunder now underscored my Dad's words. *Is God displeased with Dad's little speech or Mom's round shoulders?* In this moment he turned to me and said: "Lois, you will be next if I see you slouching again."

The air was thick and humid. Dark clouds hovered over our heads threatening the flat Delta land. Rumbles of thunder in the distance echoed as our group continued the somber march to our Sabbath meeting. It was upsetting enough that I asked myself, *Is God angry with me?*

Continuing in procession, I glanced at my mom. She winced. I remembered the non-healing sores her shoulder harness caused during the past year as she toiled in the cotton fields, washed clothes, and prepared our daily meals.

"Nobody knows the agony of wearing this brace," Mom had told me. "It causes pain in my back and neck and shoulders."

But it was The Elder's decree that she obey her spouse under any condition, and she accepted orders without a word.

"It's better than going to hell," she reasoned.

Could The Elder doom someone to hell for being round-shouldered or for daring to loosen a brace? Could he? I caught myself lest such brave rebellion — though only in thought — reach The Elder's attention and bring his merciless condemnation upon me.

Thunder continued to crack like some despotic whip as members walked — meek and stone-faced. In robotic fashion each person struggled to make footprints more perfect than the ones before them. Families walked from their separate dwellings, some just across gardens while others trudged a mile down narrow, well-beaten, dirt paths and gravel roads. They conformed to The Elder's orders by walking single file. Men walked ahead beginning with the oldest and down to the youngest, and the women followed by age "to prevent any lusting," The Elder always said.

Men dressed as usual in long-sleeved, heavy twill work shirts, denim coveralls or pants. They also wore leather work shoes. Their beards remained untrimmed, and their hair cut short. Fathers wore black felt hats, boys straw hats.

Women dressed in the usual floor-length, heavy twill, pilgrim gray jumpers designed to conceal any shape. Our blouses — as well as all coats — were trimmed with blue ribbon. Dark, navy blue socks and tennis shoes protected our feet.

The Elder demanded that we walk to meetings in total silence. Lips were sealed tightly by drawing the bottom lip in and slightly biting the inside to hold the seal and serve as a quiet reminder not to talk. On our way to the meeting that day I wanted to slip alongside my mom and tell her I understood about the pain her braces caused. I wanted to tell her I understood those twitches that always came to her talking eyes when she experienced fear in her heart. Surely she did not think The Elder had anything against her. But I said nothing.

Aunt Martha walked head bowed, shoulders stiff, and hands folded behind her back. She was having another of those aftermath headaches. I could tell. I knew it took a week to adjust to her headband. The Elder had approached her yesterday and said, "I see you're frowning again. I now sentence you to one month wearing the tight headband. You can sleep without it this time. God is watching. Now comply or you will wear it day and night for six months."

The gray headband covered her eyebrows, wrapped around her forehead, and extended up past the hairline and under the front of her matching head covering. Hidden under the back and attached behind the ears on both sides of the band, a two-inch wide, tight elastic surrounded the back of the head under the covering and helped press free all wrinkles and thoughts of ever frowning again. "Someday I will learn not to frown," Aunt Martha once told me.

Aunt Kay walked with a swollen face and eye, evidence of painful toothaches and infection. She held one hand over her mouth and cheek, attempting to keep the wind from chilling her face and accelerating the pain. She was always kind and, with her pleasant disposition, a friend to all around her.

The Elder often lectured, "If you trust The Lord, there is no need for any worldly medications, doctors, nurses, or dentists. God is the Pain Reliever and Great Healer. If you have the strong faith you need, you will be healed. If God wants you not to hurt, He will take the pain away."

On the final approach to the schoolhouse for the Sabbath meeting I noticed Grandpa looked weak as he led his wife and children. I knew the cause could be attributed to one or two-day fasts, often ordered by The Elder to make atonement for sin.

These meetings previously held in family homes — like the tradition of our Amish forefathers — now met in our colony schoolhouse. Our schoolhouse was known as a former tenant or slave house. It's called a shotgun house because of being built in one long, straight, narrow shot of rooms. It had a tin roof and it looked weathered, raw boarded, and rough. The house sat on cement blocks in the middle of a cotton field surrounded by a tiny yard of Bermuda grass.

Everyone meticulously heeded the rules before entry and formed a line in front of the *hisley* (outhouse). We prepared for the four-hour meeting. As we entered the schoolhouse, we resisted slamming the wooden screen door and any inside doors. The Elder considered any intense sound an offense.

Inside the back room we passed the cardboard wall of

The Elder's small living quarters. He always kept his door shut, and I imagined him inside on his knees praying or studying the Bible most of the time.

Extremely hot from the walk, we filed past the wash basins sitting on a wooden bench. We stopped to wash our hands, faces, and necks. On the opposite end the white granite water bucket sat with one floating, drinking dipper. Dad was the first to drink a dipper full of water. Some ran off his mustache, down his beard, and back into the water pail. According to position in line, we sipped our last water until after the meeting.

Because of The Elder's warning, as we walked through the printing room, we lifted our feet up high to prevent the offensive sound of shuffling. Then we entered the classroom at the front of the schoolhouse where insulation of flattened cardboard boxes tacked up with tin washers covered the walls and ceiling. Floors consisted of old boards worn smooth. Our few library books neatly lined the bookshelf on the northeast wall. Light entered from two small windows, one east and one west. Huge slate blackboards hung on the front and back walls displaying special Bible verses and the date. The black, wood-burning stove stood on a tin base at the center of the back wall.

With hushed precaution the members took their seats all lined up by order and position. We always faced torward north which, according to The Elder, meant toward God. I looked straight ahead, as rules required, yet my side vision told me that somber faces had lips sealed tightly in place. Insecticide sprayed on area crops saturated the air and mixed with the classroom odors of blackboard chalk and stove ashes. I heard heavy breathing and growling stomachs. Suddenly hasty steps from behind sounded heavier, grew louder, and closer as my heart pounded faster and faster.

At last the door at the back of the classroom opened and The Elder appeared. He walked briskly to the desk in front where he stood for a moment, his six-foot fragile frame dressed as always in a pilgrim gray twill, long-sleeved shirt, black corduroy pants, and a black corduroy jacket trimmed with blue ribbon. His waist length, gray hair and beard was held in place around his neck with a very large rubber band which gave his hair a page boy look. The long ends of hair and beard were tucked inside his shirt. His dull, black shoes tapped as he paced beside the teacher's desk.

Then circling the room, he walked down the aisle past me and to the back of the room. Pausing, he went up another aisle and in front to his spot beside the desk. He smelled fresh and clean — this time — after his once-a-week Friday evening bath and occasional shampooing of his hair and beard. I thought the prophet looked especially nice with his fluffy beard and hair.

"I have heard the voice of Jehovah God," he called out. "I heard His voice more clearly than ever before in all my years of divine service . . . as clearly as ever Abraham heard, or Moses, or Joshua."

The last time I heard The Elder speak with such authority, Fanny Schrock, a teenager, frantically jumped to her feet and ran out of the meeting screaming. Then we listened to her voice fade into the distance, thinking she must be the one in the group who — according to The Elder — was going to hell. Now I began to tremble and reached to touch my mom. Without taking her eyes off The Elder, she pushed my hand back. Her action made me feel uncertain.

Now once again The Elder's powerful, piercing, blue eyes smote each person as he erupted like a volcano. Molten words flowed from his lips.

"Some in here are lagging behind in good works and aren't doing their best. They are too lax and out of hand. Improve yourselves; improve I say! But there is one of you who is really in the red and of the Devil. I urge you . . . the guilty one . . . to reveal yourself. Stand up, come forth, and confess your sin now. Now, I repeat! You *will* be known today."

What could he be talking about? It couldn't be anyone in my family!

The Elder, arms folded and resting on his chest, raised his right hand to his chin and placed his index finger on his lips. After a long pause he began his usual stroking of both sides of his mustache.

"Mary Long!" he bellowed out, pointing at Mom. "Stand up and confess!"

Everyone looked on dumbstruck as Mom gasped then stumbled to her feet. For the moment she could say nothing.

"Confess!" The Elder thundered. "Jehovah God demands it!"

Large raindrops pelted the tin roof like hail, and an accusing spirit moved across the room. Had my mom, so loved and respected, so helpful to all in need, fallen into a secret sin? No one could doubt it for The Elder declared it.

"You have hidden money," The Elder said. He spoke as a judge in court. "For any chance of mercy and to be spared from eternal damnation, you must now reveal the sum and tell us where you obtained this forbidden, filthy lucre, the root of all evil. Now, confess!"

"I have no money," Mom pleaded.

The Elder's voice exploded a few notches louder and with his many words he struck Mom down like lightning.

"God is judge and in His Holy Bible He announces that all liars shall have their part in the lake of fire . . . HELL . . . and you must confess now how much money you have."

Thunder rolled and rain came in sheets. People sat frozen as condemnation poured from The Elders lips. He paused with a deadly look aimed directly at Mom.

"I don't have any . . . any money," Mom choked out again.

After this tongue lashing, the congregation sat eagle-eyed, mouths open, and in silence. *Alles vor schtill* (All was still.) Those horrifying minutes seemed like hours. The people were waiting for Mom to confess. We all knew the rule that only fathers were to handle money. Women and children were not allowed to have even a penny in their possession. Fear for Mom filled my heart as I wondered if she had done something wrong. *What was about to happen?*

Dropping into her seat, Mom put her head between her knees feeling faint once again. She told me later that she prayed silently asking the Lord if she had done or thought something wrong without knowing it to please reveal it to her then so she could confess. No answer came and she remained silent.

The Elder rebuking her again said, "I will give you twenty-four hours to write a statement of confession saying how much money you have. Mary, you will return with the statement to a special meeting here at one o'clock tomorrow. I order silence concerning the matter. This meeting is now dismissed early."

The Elder went directly to his room and shut the door. The people dispersed — speechless. There was no exchange of expressions. Silence prevailed. Each family left for their own home. My family walked out of the schoolhouse. Mom, in shock and barely able to walk the half-mile home, never said a word. Dad, with a blank look on his face, occasionally took a deep breath and swiftly kicked a rock, sending it like a torpedo into the ditch. Then he would whisper to himself.

I can still see my mom sitting atop our old cedar chest with a pencil and paper in hand, thinking, waiting, wanting to write something. Looking dazed, her helpless, blue eyes routinely stared at the paper then occasionally glanced up and peered out the window toward the schoolhouse. She looked back at the paper and prayed for the wisdom to know what to do.

Later I heard Mom say to Dad, "Clarence, I simply don't have any money."

"Yes, I know you have no money."

"What should I do?" she asked with a sigh.

"I don't know," Dad replied. "I just don't know."

"I can't put a dollar amount on this paper like I was told," Mom said. "It would be wrong and a lie if I did. It would be a sin, and I can't produce any money. I fear if I do or don't I will be sentenced for a double sin. I wonder if this is a spiritual thing or done to test my faith. I feel trapped and confused. I feel condemned to . . . to . . . HELL . . . without any escape."

The next day watching the sky, a shroud came over

me. *Why did God allow such pain on His people.* I felt extremely sorry for Mom observing the pressure I saw her under and the fear I read in her eyes almost twenty-four hours after that meeting. The rules prohibited tears and anger. No faces were to be read like an open book showing feelings in any way at any time. Seeing her, I hurt inside. *Will she ever be the same, happy Mom I knew before?* She drifted about trying to go through the motions of her daily routine, preparing meals, and doing all her duties in an artificial way — as she did for many following days.

I could not keep from wondering if there was something I did not know and if I would lose my Mom in some way. *Could she actually go to hell because of this? Would she survive the ordeal?* She looked as though she gave up on living.

I whispered to Dad, "What will happen to us children and you if we lose Mom?"

He began talking to himself, communicating with his spirit world in low tones but never answering me. Since his nervous breakdown, we knew Dad was neither mentally stable nor capable of caring for my brother, Fred, my sister, Joan, and me.

Twenty-four hours later, by The Elder's decree, Mom went to her scheduled meeting — alone. I watched as she left home trembling, walking slowly down that narrow, gravel road. I knew how much she dreaded each footstep. I knew she prayed all the way to the schoolhouse that the truth would prevail. Only three other people — selected by The Elder — were allowed at this meeting. The rest of my family forced themselves to stay home and pray. I looked out our east window and waited with anticipation believing that something would be worked out. What was being said and done behind those walls and closed doors? I felt certain the facts would surface and Mom would be relieved and set free again.

Finally Mom came out the back door and collapsed to the ground behind the schoolhouse. She sat by herself for a long while. Not a good sign, or was it? Were The Elder and the other people inside considering the truth, forgiveness, and Mom's reinstatement?

A deep sigh within my spirit, hands grasping the sill, and my nose on the window pane half thinking she could hear me, I whispered, "Mom, Mom, what can I do? I want to be with you. Are you all right? Why aren't you getting up? Are you hurt? I want to help you, but I can't without The Elder's permission or a curse might be put on me."

I knew her pain. I could feel it. Mom struggled to her feet, stood for a moment looking toward home, and then slowly walked to us. Her head covering rippled and her floor-length dress snapped in the wind. Her head hung down, down, way down low.

Dad, disturbed, whispered to himself and paced the floor quickly from one end of our old shotgun house to the other. We children quietly watched out the east window as Mom came nearer and nearer.

Mom came silently into our front room and sat on a wooden bench. Her face was blank. After a lapse of time she stated in a shaky voice, "I'm doomed to hell now. I'm doomed. *Doomed forever!*"

Chapter 11

Childhood in the Colony

I was called Patricia Ann Long when I joined Lael Colony in the Tennessee Valley shortly after my fourth birthday. To me this place looked like a paradise on earth. As we entered the east gate, huge trees waved their arms and walled the narrow dirt road. Natural springs bubbled. Creeks wound through the 2,005 acres. Warm air softly swept the quiet meadows and hills. Far away cottony clouds floated across the blue sky. I wondered, *is this the Garden of Eden I've heard adults talking about?*

Passing my great Uncle Christian's house, we finally arrived at my Miller grandparent's home. Two Grandparents, seven aunts, five uncles, several great aunts and uncles, and many cousins eagerly welcomed my family. We were finally in Lael Colony.

A few weeks later I experienced one of the first surprises about this place, our new home.

Dressed in his black corduroy suit and black felt hat, The Elder was a bit frightening to a four year old. His piercing blue eyes followed me as I walked into the room with Mom and Dad. The Elder spoke with deep solemnity. "Clarence, you will no longer call this child Patricia. From this time on you must call her Lois."

Never having heard the name Lois before, I whispered to Daddy, "Why?"

"Listen and you'll find out. Just listen," Daddy said softly with raised eyebrows.

I felt unsure if I should feel sad from a loss or thrilled with a gain. The Elder saw me as an infant when my parents

113

visited the colony years ago, but I didn't feel as if I knew him much at all. He was a stranger to me. I spoke few words to him as I stood between my parents and looked around Mom's light blue apron.

With his eyes fixed on me, The Elder continued. "God has spoken to me, and you are chosen to have a good Bible name. The name Patricia is too worldly. People will be tempted to call you Patty and that wouldn't be good." Turning to Mom he said, "Mary, read to her about Lois in the Bible, 2 Timothy 1:5-7. Your daughter should try her best to live up to being like this holy woman."

Then looking back at me he declared, "Lois, is your name. Lois, you must learn Ephesians 6:1-3, in the King James Version. *Children obey your parents in the Lord; for this is right. Honor thy father and mother which is the first commandment with promise, that it may be well with thee, and that thou mayest live long on the earth.* You obey your parents now. That will please the Lord, and you will be doing good."

Mom read and explained to me the scripture from 2 Timothy that The Elder had mentioned. I listened intently. "But Mommy, why should I be called her name?"

"You have always been my *why* child. Now you see your new name is supposed to be special and chosen, like a good lady in the Bible. What a privilege!" Mom insisted. "The Elder has changed several others names, too, not just yours."

"Whose?"

"Well, my sister, your Aunt Rosie's name was changed to Naomi. And The Elder gave your Aunt Martha a middle name, San, which in Hebrew means saint, and that's good."

"Did he just change girl's names?"

"No. The Elder gave different names to my brothers, your uncles that are nearly your age. Uncle Ed's was changed to Besodiah, a Bible name. My family had called Benjamin, Daniel, to keep from getting his name mixed up with Grandpa's. But the Elder said to call him Benjamin not Daniel. Now we call him Benja for short. He gave your Uncle Micah a middle name, Enoch. Some of your cousin's names were changed too. Howard was re-named Gad, and Hannah was to be called April."

"I know Hannah's in the Bible, so that's a Bible name. Why did The Elder change her name to April, a calendar name?"

"I don't know!" Mom answered quickly for she never wanted to try to explain anything The Elder did or didn't do. "It's settled. Now we will call you Lois."

"Okay, Mommy, but I never heard the name Patty. Who's that?"

"Some people named Patricia are called Patty for short, but we never called you that. The Elder is concerned that somebody might, and he says it would not be good."

"But Mommy, if my name changes, will I stay the same?"

"It's up to you. Do you think you will change?"

"I want to grow big and learn a lot."

"You will!" Mom assured and added, "Now, Lois, you should help everybody remember to call you by your new good name, Lois."

"Okay!" Then I whispered, "Mommy, I really want to be like you and like Grandmother Lois in the Bible. I will obey and be good all the time."

"That's great, and it will please everyone," Mom said. "You are the most optimistic child I've ever seen."

"What does optimistic mean?"

"It means you see the bright and good side of everything all the time and that's good."

Looking back, I must have been like a pains-taking questionnaire, filled with curiosity which tested my parent's patience. The next two years changed me. My curiosity and desire to know about everything didn't change, but I lost the freedom to ask any questions I thought of. No one seemed willing to even try to answer my innumerable questions.

"You don't question what I say. It's from the Lord just like Moses' words. And children don't question what your parents say! Just obey them like the Bible says." The Elder issued those orders repeatedly. "The quieter you are the less chances of sinning. So seal your lips as much as possible."

This made many questions and thoughts flow through my mind without ever leaking out.

At first my family often forgot to call me Lois. My job was to remember and remind others to call me by my good name. I reminded Grandpa, Fred, and Joan the most. I recall not responding to Lois at first, but I was strictly reminded to answer when I'm called. Sometimes I answered to either name. Soon I became Lois to everyone in the colony and never heard Patricia again. I learned to spell Lois and was happy with my new name. For eleven years of my life Lois remained my name.

Little did I know then that this was the beginning of the birdcage childhood I would live for the next twelve years. Neither did I know that my life would someday shrink tight into a ball of nothing called rock bottom. Rock bottom doesn't even describe how I felt after my mom was excommunicated. I had no idea how the tentacles of change were about to reach out and ensnare me.

About six months later when I was fifteen, The Elder called my teacher aside and gave her new orders. "You must call Lois, Patricia. From now on her name will be changed back to Patricia," The Elder instructed. "And you are to send a note to her parents of this order."

When I heard that my Bible name was taken away and my heathen name restored, I felt crushed like a smashed dish under a ton of stones. My heart cried out inside without showing a tear. *Why? Why do I have to be called a name that The Elder had declared a heathen worldly name? And I don't even know how to spell that worldly name. What have I done to deserve losing my good Bible name? I don't believe I am in the red (bad) or have done anything wrong! Why did The Elder decide to do this?*

My parents seemed disappointed, yet they obeyed the orders. This didn't feel right or good to me. Dad appeared angry and refused to call me Patricia. Instead he called me Tricia, or Tish. Mom tried to reason with me, and she called me Patricia like the rest of the colony. My brother and sister called me Trish.

Childhood in the Colony

"The Elder must feel there is a sin in the family. That's probably why he ordered your name changed back to Patricia," Mom explained. "I don't believe it has anything to do with you personally being good or bad. I believe he feels I am the bad one in our family. I'm the one he excommunicated. I'm the one he doomed to hell."

This made sense to me that The Elder would do that, and I cringed to think, *my mom will burn in hell forever. But why do I have to take a punishment for something Mom's falsely accused of doing?* Each time somebody called me Patricia it felt painful, worse than a slap in the face or one of my severe toothaches. *Will I be Patricia for the rest of my life? I believe The Elder will give my good name back to me someday if this is not my fault. I will be patient and wait on the Lord. We certainly often wrote 'Wait on the Lord' for our school writing assignments.*

My world was collapsing. My dreams were shattered. I crashed wondering who I really was. My identity was stolen! Who was I? Who would I become? The pain and fractures took time to heal.

This last name change was a culmination of years of anxiety and broke open buried heartaches. There was nothing in my world to offer hope.

Three things were paramount to me. My mother's excommunication, my name change, and my dad's strange behavior.

Dad always seemed busy and occupied within himself, and he seldom heard me when I spoke to him. Caught up in his own world, he always lagged behind while hoeing and picking cotton. We helped him keep up by hoeing long spaces and picking cotton in long areas of his row. I never held him responsible for anything he said or did. I believed he cared about us but could not show it.

I know Dad took it very seriously when I almost died from an unknown illness at the age of ten. I could hear him and Mom discuss my physical condition, and finally in desperation he went to The Elder for advice.

"There's sin in Lois' life or her family for this to happen," The Elder told him. "If she has enough faith or her family has enough faith, she'll live and if not she'll die. Now Clarence, you go home and pray!"

Dad was helpless. No one questioned The Elder. Yet Dad had to return home to his sick and failing child. Was her death inevitable?

Dad came into my room and sat on the side of my bed. "Lois," he spoke my name softly. I was unable to answer, but I slowly recovered knowing God had spared my life.

I never heard Dad or Mom say, "I love you" and they never kissed or hugged each other or their children. That would have broken the rules about the use of the worldly word "love" or to show affection. *If he broke anger rules, why couldn't he break love rules?* I wondered. He often showed anger, and we knew to stay out of his path.

Growing up I never knew how miserable Dad was; yet I never heard him swear. He never spoke of his childhood, his service in the Marine Corps, or of his imprisoned father. The Elder's instructions not to laugh angered Dad. Yet he complied.

When the cotton fields were too wet to work in, I liked going with Dad to cut firewood. He seemed to enjoy woodcutting more than the fieldwork. We packed lunch, took Shag along, and as a family we cut firewood all day. This seemed more relaxing than working in the fields for pay. Dad and Mom usually were not quite as strict about working every minute, but there was not much idle time.

"Lois and Joan, quit messing around with Shag or he'll stay home tomorrow. Now get those branches and brush out of the way," Dad echoed. "Children stay busy and work hard if you want to be warm this winter. Remember what the The Elder said, 'never have idle hands.' Remember idle hands are the Devils trap, so keep your hands as busy as when you pick cotton."

"Is it almost lunch time?" Fred asked hopefully.

"If it were, I'd tell you," Dad snapped. "Now shake that lazy man off your back and get to work. Remember the Devil is as a roaring lion seeking to devour you. Now work so fast the Devil can't catch you and ride your back."

Childhood in the Colony

No one said a word.

Dad knew how to fall a tree. Set an acorn target and Dad was sure to crush that very acorn with a huge tree. He used an axe with great skill for cutting firewood. His knowledge of the tools and the forest came from summers he spent as a teenager cutting timber for his uncle in Oregon. Mom, Fred, Joan and I helped cut up trees and pile brush and wood. We used large crosscut saws, bow saws, axes, hatches, sledges, wedges and manpower to cut wood.

Occasionally Dad suffered with toothaches. I saw his face swollen once and knew it slowed him down and made him irritable. I could understand his misery. The time I saw his face swell up the worst he had robbed honeybees in the wall of our house. He wore his straw hat and put netting over it tying the netting at his neck. He tore boards off our house and pulled large honeycombs out while the bees swarmed in furry. They stung his neck where the netting was held close with a rubber band. His throat and face swelled. Nevertheless we had dishpans of good honey from that harvest.

Another time a flash rain made the cotton too wet to pick, and that forced us out of the field. Then the sun came out and Dad took us fishing in the bayou. Along the bank we cut bamboo for poles, tied lines on them, added hooks, sinkers, bait, and sometimes a stick bobber. We only caught catfish and one eel that day. I surely didn't want to catch another eel; it put up a big fight and acted and looked too much like a snake. We learned how to cast into the water without catching on trees or the bayou banks so often.

"Throw it back!" Dad shouted each time that we caught something. "We're not allowed to eat catfish. They have fins but no scales. All fish we eat must have fins and scales according to The Elder and the Old Testament dietary laws."

Fred and I went fishing again but only caught catfish. I recall getting stung by one which seemed worse than bumblebee stings. This reduced my desire to fish in the bayou where mostly catfish lived. It seemed hard to get them off the hook without getting stung or hurting the fish's mouth.

Dad promised to take us fishing in a real lake someday. He said a lake is where we could catch fish with fins and scales that we could eat, but he never took us. I recalled before we left Indiana that he had promised to take us for a train ride, but he never did that either. I always wondered what a train ride would have been like and what it would be like to fish in a real lake.

A special memory I have of Dad is another time when we were rained out of the cotton field. "Lois, you're going with me to town now," Dad ordered. "Today I'll buy you a pair of shoes that fit."

"Am I allowed to go to town?" I asked, looking at Mom. Dad made no comment.

"You obey you father!" Mom said. "I have ordered from Sears catalog and returned two or three pairs of shoes for you that didn't fit. This might be a quick way to get you shoes to wear. You know there's frost on the ground every morning now, and you are still going barefoot like its summer. You need shoes!"

Going to town seemed far beyond my wildest, scary dreams. The idea that I might see town, stores, and outside people or they see me sounded scary. We were taught to never be heard nor seen by strangers if possible. That's why we hid if a car came down the road when we were working in our yard or garden. At age eleven this was my only childhood trip to town while living in the colony.

When we arrived in town, people stared at me as if they saw a freak. Complete amazement fell over me when I saw the grocery store and how much food was stacked everywhere. I guess I had no idea of how it might look where food was sold. I saw many unbelievably strange things and people.

"Follow me!" Dad ordered. "Just follow me!" I followed Dad and people seemed to follow me looking with big white eyes surrounded by dark skin.

On this trip Dad bought me nice, new, navy tennis shoes in the dime store. At the check out I tapped Dad and pointed to a small white handled, pocket knife only one and a half inches long with a tiny chain on one end. "Fred would like that," I whispered.

"I'll buy it for *you*," Dad said.

Dad told the cashier to get the knife, and I believe he paid no more than a dollar for it. He handed the tiny knife to me. In disbelief I held it tight.

I felt totally shocked and overwhelmed at all the new and unusual stuff. I was especially surprised when Dad bought me something other than a pair of shoes. Knives were considered boys stuff and needles and crochet hooks were for girls. *Should I feel guilty? Am I sinning or breaking any of The Elder's rules? Am I obeying my Father?* Nevertheless I tightly held the tiny knife in the palm of my hand, occasionally glancing at it in disbelief. I wondered, *Did Dad buy this knife for me because of all the times he restricted me from having sweets?*

Going home I sat silent and listened as Dad talked to himself. This was the first time I remember my dad ever buying me anything besides shoes, food, or fabric to make clothes. It was my first knife. Awestruck, my eyes stayed busy capturing every view between the sky and the ground, strange people, houses, cars, country roads, and animals. Excitement welled up inside me once I realized we were on the gravel road near home. Flashing in my mind, *what will Fred say when he sees my knife?*

Once home, I ran to Fred and opened my hand. "See what Dad bought me! Thinking he might buy it for you, I told Dad that you would like this knife. I was surprised when he said he would buy it for me. I'm a girl and I'm not to have a boy's knife. Here, you take it."

"That's really a cute little knife," Fred said. "I'd keep it if I were you. It's too small to use for the rough things I do, and I have two brown pocketknives. I'm glad he bought it for you. You keep it!"

I used the small knife to rip out seams when sewing. I treasured the tiny knife all my childhood, and I still have it today.

At times Dad brought home free, wooden, apple boxes from the grocery, but never any apples because he couldn't afford to buy them. We used the boxes for seats, storage shelves, and to store stuff. He made each of us a tiny desk from an apple box by moving one side into the middle, turning the box on its side, and putting legs on it. This was the only piece of furniture I owned, and I highly valued my apple box desk. It stood beside the head of my bed most of my childhood. This is where I kept my highly valued treasures like my Bible, Scripture Line Book, El-Elohe-Israel book, a book I typed in school, crochet hooks, knitting needles, and the 'learn how' books.

I found blessings in my dad despite his problems. Years later he would say, "The Lord never let me enjoy my children. He tortured me with a special kind of communication with Him and people around the world."

My childhood was filled with varied memories.

Chapter 12

School Days

My school days began at Lael Parochial School in Lael Valley near Iron City, Tennessee. Our private one room school, for Lael Colony members only, was run by the colony and under strict instructions, rules, and scrutiny of The Elder.

Our teacher, Ms. Delilah Miller, was appointed by The Elder and on his orders she was only called Dee. She was my great aunt, Grandpa Miller's sister. Dee, barely five feet tall, round faced, brown eyed, brunette, super energetic and courageous, was an enthusiastic and witty lady in her early thirties. With only an eighth grade education she taught first through eighth grades. She had previously taught in the Amish school and the colony school in Hamilton, Mississippi.

Colony members built our schoolhouse from timber they harvested in Lael Valley. They cut trees, made raw lumber, and dried it at the saw mill. They built the schoolhouse with only one door to the west. Several small windows on the south, east, and west sides lit the large room. Later they added The Elder's room on the north side. The outside was covered with black tarpaper held up by round metal washers with a nail in the center.

Some of the inside walls were raw wood, and some were covered with flattened cardboard boxes. Two large blackboards hung on the north wall near the teacher's desk. A black, wood burning stove stood by the west wall mid-way between the door and the teacher's desk. About thirty desks lined up in rows filled the room.

Our desks were old, used, wooden desks with names and alphabets carved on them and an ink bottle hole at the top right side. We primarily used pencils, but each student had one refillable ink pen. I still have my one and only very precious, green, refillable ink pen.

The Elder lived in Dee's small trailer behind the schoolhouse until the room he ordered built onto the back of the schoolhouse was finished. At recess when we walked past the open door to The Elder's room, I recall my mouth watering when I saw his special ordered bananas lying on his desk. He never offered students any. I remembered the taste of bananas I had when I lived in Indiana, and I don't believe I ever had any again until I returned to Indiana years later.

At age four I started school after The Elder, the teacher, and my parents evaluated me and decided to start me in first grade with Fred. Fred, eleven months older than I, was five. Years later, I asked Mom why they put me in first grade at age four years and two months.

"They didn't have kindergarten at Lael Parochial, and I told them if Fred was ready for school so were you because Fred had learned to say a lot of words from you," Mom said. "Many of the children, like the Amish, started in first grade at seven, but they felt you and Fred were ready even though you were much younger. The Elder ordered us to put you in school at age four, so we did. You were the youngest in the school that year."

I remember saying all the ABC's and counting to 100 when they evaluated me. I really enjoyed my first year of school. I learned to read from the Dick and Jane readers and to spell three and four letter words. I learned to add and subtract and was not satisfied with any grade less than an A+. In the afternoon when my work was done, I recall Dee saying, "Lois, you're tired. Lay your head on your desk and take a ten to fifteen minute nap, and then I will wake you."

After that short nap I always felt better. She also let me lay my head on my desk when I had a toothache. Fred's desk was right beside mine in the first row at the front of the room near the teacher's desk. There were about 30 students in the school that year.

School Days

When Fred and I walked to school, Mom walked with us to the first bend in the dirt, timber road. Then she watched us walk to the second bend, and our teacher or the older students watched for us to come around that bend, always at the same time. They watched us after school in reverse order. Poisonous snakes, especially rattlers, lying on the road was a big concern, but we had plenty of warnings to watch for them.

At times Dee appointed older students to help younger ones. I recall getting helped by Aunt Kay, one of those students. I liked to go to the pencil sharpener on the wall to sharpen my dull pencils. The students were never allowed to mess around or play. Following the work ethic The Elder taught, we only had time for working on lessons or studying.

Dee tried to help the students enjoy learning. One special time she had all the students trace a six-inch boat pattern on paper, cut it out, and glue the three corners together. "If you do a good job, your boat will float. If not, it will sink," Dee said, "so do your best, and I will have a surprise for you." We let the boats dry over night.

The next day at recess our surprise was the opportunity to see if our boats would sink or float. Two students at a time put their boats into Swanagan Branch Creek behind the schoolhouse. I thought this was fun watching our boats float down the stream, and I saw some of them sink. Mine stayed afloat as far as I could see. What an experience this was for me. The boats floated off around the creek bend — gone forever — without a chance of ever playing with them.

The Elder got wind of this experiment — likely from hearing the chatter of excited children — and he put a stop to it and all boat making. This brief glimpse of 'fun schoolwork' felt good. I overheard somebody ask if it was evil. I assume The Elder thought so. He stopped it.

Another time Dee gave each student a cigar box to cover and use for their pencil box or their special things. She helped them cover their boxes with paper or fabric. No worldly words, pictures, or stuff was to be on anything we had.

This was a good and happy school year for me in first

grade. However at the end of that year The Elder excommunicated Dee, our teacher. This news wounded my heart and stung the hearts of many children. *How could this be? I liked Dee for my teacher.* Now The Elder called her a skunk and a wicked woman, like Jezebel in the Bible.

"Students return everything that wicked woman gave you," The Elder ordered. "I mean *everything* down to the smallest thing you can find. This will prevent a curse on you. Abraham Schrock, you haul that skunk out of this village, out of this valley, and completely off this land. Then set all the skunk's buildings on fire and burn them to the ground. Burn all those books she taught from for they are contaminated. Students, carry all the schoolbooks to the saw mill and burn them. That evil woman and all her contamination and stuff will be out of here."

As a young child, I was convinced my first teacher was evil and would burn in hell. The only signs that Dee was ever a part of Lael Valley were the two piles of ashes from her house and shed. *I'll never see her again,* I thought. This hurt me as a four-year-old to think something so terrible could happen to my nice teacher and aunt. This left fear and a sinkhole in my heart for years. *What if. . . . How could they? Why?* That was the end of my first school year.

The Elder appointed my mother's oldest sister, Aunt Naomi, as the teacher for the next school year. Naomi, five feet three inches, and very thin, blue eyed, light brown hair, rather quiet and insecure, expressed her feelings of inadequacy, yet she could not refuse to comply. She, too, had an eighth grade education. Before the next school year under orders from The Elder my family left Lael Valley, and my next school year was in Mississippi.

Years later several students who remained in Lael Valley for the next school year told me about a one inch snow fall, an unusual event for there in Tennessee. At recess the schoolboys, delighted by their very first snow, gleefully rolled a big snowball. The mood changed quickly when The Elder saw it. "Roll that snowball into the creek right now," he ordered wide-eyed. "Never let this kind of horseplay happen again."

The student's excitement ended quickly. More rules were added to the growing list of 'Do's and Don'ts.'

Dissatisfaction and unrest was increasing. Finally the colony split. Some remained in Lael Valley, and some moved to the cotton plantation on the Mississippi Delta. Our family was among the first that The Elder sent there, and I attended the temporary school at Uncle Eli Miller's home. Uncle Eli was Grandpa Miller's brother. His wife, Aunt Maude, having less than an eighth grade education, was appointed by The Elder as our temporary teacher in Mississippi. Uncle Eli's living room became the classroom for the seven students.

This was the time my family temporarily lived with Uncle Eli, Aunt Maude, and their four children. I enjoyed living with Uncle Eli. Their four children were older than my siblings and I. I liked their friendly dog, Tan, and their cat, Tiger.

Soon we moved to the snake den house. To get from there to school at Uncle Eli's we walked at least one mile down a cotton field, dirt road, across a cow pasture, and through a bayou and woods. Even though the bayou was often difficult to cross, even harder and more scary for me was getting through the cow pasture when the cows and the bull were standing near our path. We tried to avoid this danger by dashing behind trees to keep the bull from butting us. We knew to run for a tree when the bull's tail went up, his head down, and he pawed and charged toward us with fury. Creeping around a big tree was our only defense other than climbing up a small tree and waiting for the bull to leave. If the bull lingered too long, we were late for school.

Sometimes we accidentally stepped in a cow paddy and fell, leaving us smelling like manure. Often we were wet from morning dew and muddy from falling down. Once at school we removed our muddy shoes or boots. Our clothes eventually dried.

The Elder ordered Uncle David, Mom's oldest brother, to move from his restrictions in Tennessee and into the greater confinement at Uncle Eli's. He was permitted out of the house only after dark. The Elder had ordered him to confinement to prevent military officials from finding him because he was draft age. The Elder instructed him and the colony not to let anybody know he existed.

I enjoyed our ten minute visits with him after school. That was a special time for us and for Uncle David. He was always kind and friendly to us. We caught *mooka* in his windows each day and put them outside.

At mid school year we moved from the snake den house to the shotgun house under the big oak tree where I would live for the next ten years. About that time The Elder released Grandpa Miller's family from the Tennessee Valley and they moved to the Mississippi Delta cotton plantation. Uncle David then moved from Uncle Eli's and lived with his own family. I missed visiting with Uncle David after school.

Later The Elder moved from Tennessee and lived at Uncle Eli's in the room where Uncle David and my family had stayed.

From our home under the big oak tree we walked across the gravel road, through one cow pasture, passed an old barn, walked alongside another cow pasture, over a field, and then down Uncle Eli's long, dirt lane. We enjoyed the walk from our oak tree house to Uncle Eli's much more than from the snake den house. As usual we were ordered to walk single file, oldest to youngest, and not deviate from that order except to help each other.

We helped each other through barbed wire fences by one pulling up on one strand and pushing down on the bottom strand while another crawled through. We still occasionally snagged and ripped holes in our clothes. Sometimes we were distracted by wild, barn cats and their kittens and walked slow to see them run.

When the field was plowed, we sometimes became stuck in the mud and had to pull each other out. There is nothing like Mississippi mud. When it rained and was wet enough, we sunk knee deep into the freshly plowed field. As that mud dried to clay, it stuck to our boots giving us monstrous feet. Many times we had to stop and clean the caked mud off our shoes and boots because they became so heavy we couldn't walk or the weight would pull our boots and shoes off our feet. Occasionally carefree we leisurely walked to school and enjoyed it, mud and all, knowing no mean bull would threaten us on this path where only the nice cows watched us.

Between the time Uncle David moved from Uncle Eli's and The Elder moved in there was the worst time for me. I became the school sinner. On the way to school one sunny day the mud packed on our feet till we couldn't lift them, and we stopped to clean the mud off. I pulled a piece of clay like mud from my boot and squashed it in my hand as I walked. Soon without thinking much I squeezed the mud between my thumb and index finger. A small, round, head-shaped clump of mud popped out. I shaped two small arms. Then I molded two legs, and I had a three-inch mud baby doll with arms and legs and a head and no face. *She would make a nice friend for a corncob doll,* I thought.

I wrapped the mud doll in my light blue handkerchief and held it in my hand. The more I looked at it as I walked to school the more I liked it. I knew we were not to play with dolls, yet I wanted a baby doll so much even if I couldn't play with it. To have one was good enough even if I had to hide it till I went home. I put it in my pocket before I walked into our schoolroom and sat at my desk. To prevent the mud doll from getting smashed, I decided to put it way in the back of my desk behind all the books until I went home. It was fine until recess. I wanted to have one peek at the doll. I must have given it too much attention because my teacher, Aunt Maude, came back to me and asked, "What do you have in your desk?"

"Books," I said as my heart pounded in my ears. I remained silent as my teacher jerked my desk up on its two front legs. She began pulling all the books out and laying them on my lap. I knew she would find my baby doll in the back. *What will happen?* This thought flooded my mind with great fear. When she came to my small blue handkerchief, she pulled it out, opened it, and with one look her eyes became saucers of fire. Aunt Maude exploded into a fury.

"You made an idol in the likeness of God," Aunt Maude snorted. "You broke one of the Ten Commandments."

I was speechless! I literally felt nearly shamed to death and scared as a scolded pup. *Now what will happen to me? Will I be hauled off and dumped far away like Joseph, my cousin?* Aunt Maude would not even touch the unclean idol as she called my mud doll.

"I must put this evil idol you have made outside and save it for evidence. It's too evil to be in our classroom," my teacher shouted. "I order you to go home after school and tell your parents. Then you must return with your father to decide your punishment."

Fear overwhelmed me for the rest of that day.

Once home, I told my parents. Dad immediately took me back to school. This was my most dreadful school visit ever.

"Clarence, Lois is a sinner in our midst," Aunt Maude shouted as we approached. "She made a graven image in the likeness of God and brought it into the classroom. This is contrary to Bible teachings in. . . ." She couldn't think of the Scripture reference but with waving arms and big flashing button eyes she squealed wildly, "Lois should be severely punished for this evil and sinful act. And I will get the evidence."

She walked around the outside of the house and brought the wrapped evidence. Opening the handkerchief, she showed Dad my mud doll. More condemning words rolled from her full lips. I can still see in my mind's eye how she stood and bounced around spiting out more words. Then she rose up on her tip toes and reaching up as high as she could and with my mud baby doll in her hand she thrust it to the brick walk with such force that the doll shattered into a million pieces before my eyes. My dad had no room to speak a word for the air was filled with condemnation from my teacher's mouth.

"I have destroyed the wicked idol. Now tell me exactly what will be Lois' punishment for committing this evil act?"

Aunt Maude demanded.

"I'll punish her at home," my dad said. "You took care of the doll. I'll take care of her." My dad turned to leave and Aunt Maude insisted to know what my punishment would be. Dad assured her that he would inflict enough punishment that I would never do it again. He walked away, and I followed him. As she watched us leave, I knew she hated me with every bone and thread of flesh in her body, mind, and soul. I felt worse than terrible. *What can I do now to repent? How can I let everybody know that I didn't plan to play with the doll? I don't know anything about graven images. I feel trapped by Aunt Maude's anger and maybe Dad's too.*

Dad whispered to himself as we walked home and never said a word to me. What nobody knew was that I had a corncob with stick arms and legs and some corn silk on top but no face. It was wrapped in a handkerchief and hidden under the hay in our barn. After I had made the mud doll, I thought, *it will be nice if my corncob doll has company.* That's why I tried to keep the mud doll.

I knew I couldn't play with them, but on the Sabbath Day I could sit in the hay and read the Bible to both dolls. I had been doing this with the corncob doll when I studied my Bible verses. *My mud doll is gone, but what will happen if anybody finds my corncob doll hidden in the hay,* I wondered. Guilt pounded on me with each step home, and I heart-cried all the way knowing better than to show a tear. *What about my corncob baby doll? Nobody will ever find her,* I thought. *And she'll never have the mud doll for her friend. She'll be alone every week and only see me on the Sabbath.*

Once home and inside the front door, Dad said, "Lois, stand in that corner on one foot for the rest of the evening till bedtime, and then go to bed. Keep your nose in the corner and don't look back or you will go to jail." I kept my nose in the corner and switched feet standing on one foot at a time. It seemed I stood in the corner half a day or more — likely four to six hours.

My stomach growled and my head ached as many thoughts flooded my mind. *Am I so bad that Dad and The*

Elder will decide to haul me to another state far away and dump me as trash like they did Joseph and as Dad did my real doll? My first teacher was condemned to hell. Will I be the first student condemned to hell for breaking the Ten Commandments? I actually made an idol in the likeness of God. An image! Guilt riddled me as I stood on one foot facing that corner. At that time I decided that I would unwrap my corncob doll from my handkerchief and take her out of hiding in the hay.

Early the next morning I went out to feed the chickens and pigeons, and I removed my corncob doll from the hay and from my handkerchief. I took the stick arms and legs off and put her back in the barn by the corn sheller where I often shelled corn and ground corn meal.

I had never played with the corncob doll. I only read to her. I had not planned ahead to make the mud doll. I had never heard of anybody making a mud doll before. I just had a piece of mud, clay-like in consistency, that came off my boot. I started squeezing it in my hand as I walked along. Suddenly I had a mud doll. Then thinking of my corncob doll, I wanted to keep the mud doll for her friend, and I wrapped it in my handkerchief and put it in my pocket. I feared it would squash so I put it in my desk until time to go home. Then all this trouble erupted. *Why was this so bad when in Tennessee I had a real doll that I could make clothes for and try them on her?*

Shortly after we moved to Mississippi, Dad gave my real doll and all the clothes I sewed for her to some African American girls he saw playing in a yard several miles outside the cotton plantation. Dad dumped my real baby doll there, and I would never see her again. I missed her and often wondered what happened to her and all the clothes that I made for her. *Did those girls take good care of her and make her more clothes?* I wondered. I couldn't sew clothes for her any more. When I told Mom I missed my doll, she said it was better this way because it would be more pleasing to God. I accepted that. I guess missing my doll is why I had the corncob wrapped as a make believe doll. When I accidentally discovered the mud molded nicely, I must have been thinking of my missing doll. This was a tough lesson for me as a little girl, yet I wanted to do the best and be the best I could.

The Elder kept an eye on the school and students. He must have watched us walking to and from school. He summoned a meeting with my parents.

"Your children are acting like little imps of Satan walking to school," The Elder scolded. "You must control those little imps of Satan and make sure they don't stop, mess around, or fall down on the path to and from school. They are to follow these strict rules and not get side tracked by anything. Walk single file by age, boy first. No stopping, holding hands, or touching each other. Each is to stand alone and yet stay together."

My parents, especially Mom, were puzzled. "Why did The Elder call our children imps of Satan at their young ages?" Mom asked Dad before talking to her mother.

Dad whispered to himself without a response to her.

"I don't understand why The Elder calls Fred, Lois, and Joan little imps of Satan," Grandma Miller said when she learned of the incident. "*Sie sinn bessa behaft on de Enoch, Besodiah, and Benja.*" (They behave better than Enoch, Besodiah, and Benja.)

Mom encouraged us to do our best to be good while walking to school.

"I will be watching as well as The Elder," Mom warned. "Most importantly God will see everything you do and hear everything you say."

I thought that maybe The Elder called us imps of Satan because sometimes we bent over looking for kittens under the barn. We also walked slow watching for the mother cat to run. Mom could see us most of the way and told us to help each other through the barred wire fences and mud, and we were obeying her. Our teacher could see us from the barn to school. We never really knew why The Elder called us little imps of Satan, and yet we knew we better walk the straight and narrow path.

We stopped to pull each other out of the mud, get through barred wire fences, and clean off our boots. There was a time that we held hands to walk through the muddiest area of the field so if one fell down, the others could help them. We even tried to stay single file holding hands. Maybe we held hands beyond the worst mud spot. I don't remember. Nevertheless The Elder had us condemned as the Devil's children. The mud was so bad that once Dad had to help Mom because she was stuck in the muddy field walking that path to a Sabbath meeting.

We got over those disappointments and tried to do our best to walk the straight and narrow path of life, the righteous way, and be perfect little children of God and not the Devil.

After hoeing and picking cotton that spring, summer, and fall, I was eager to start school with Aunt Naomi as my new teacher. Lael Parochial School was set up in a three-room, shotgun house, an old plantation slave house, which sat on blocks in the middle of a field. This schoolhouse had a front porch, a real red brick chimney, and long narrow windows that slid up to open. Our members added wooden screen doors to help airflow and keep flies out.

The front porch held our muddy boots and wet or dirty shoes while we were in school until The Elder gave this order: "There shall be no footwear left on the porch showing the number of people inside. Nobody is to sit or stand around or on the porch because somebody might drive by and see them. Boots are to be taken off at the back door and placed in the middle room closet."

The large front room served as our classroom. Rows of student desks and one teacher's desk packed the room with only narrow aisles between them. A black wood-burning stove stood at the back of the room. The walls and ceiling were covered with opened cardboard boxes nailed up with the tin washers and a nail. The floors were old boards worn smooth by slaves and share croppers. The middle room held school supplies, an old Royal typewriter, a duplicator, and printing materials. The Elder lived in one-half of the back room behind a cardboard wall. The other half had a wash basin and water bucket setting on a wooden table. A walkway ran along the side of the house from front to the back door.

Our classroom had one small shelf of library books on the east wall behind the student reading bench near the teacher's desk. The teacher's desk was near the north wall between the library books and front door in the northeast corner. On the north wall between the front door and west wall there was a wall size card rack where we wrote Bible verses with alphabet cards. Above the card rack was a place for the date and a message for the day like "Be of good courage." Each day a new Bible verse was on the board.

Along the west wall were desks. Each student sat according to The Elders placement. The boys were first by age. On the west wall, my brother's desk sat in front near the card rack, and he sat in the seat on the front of my desk. My desk sat beside the west window. I liked my view out the window until the hot afternoon sun beat in and nearly scorched me. In the winter I nearly froze from wind blowing in the cracks around the window. Pulling the shade to keep hot sun and cold winds out helped. I never wanted to chance missing any activity outside like wild animals in the cotton field or a bird on the shed roof. I even liked to see the sky and clouds. I could see my home across the bayou bridge and see our pigeons flying around our barn. If my mom was in the yard, I saw her hanging clothes on the line or working in the garden. I sat in the chair attached to the front of my sister's desk. I really hoped The Elder would never change this arragement.

On the south wall hung a huge slate blackboard with the alphabets written on top and a good message under them. There were some double rows of desks in the center of the room. All students faced north toward God as The Elder put it. Our teacher faced south. *Why did she have to face the Devil?* On the south wall after the blackboard was the black, pot bellied, wood stove with a poker and shovel under it and an ash bucket behind it. Past the stove was the door leading to the middle room, also called the printing room. Most of the printing stuff was on a bench built especially for it.

The Elder lived in the back room and kept an eye on

everybody and everything. Our school was quiet. Of course nobody was allowed to laugh, yell, or talk loud at any time even out of school. We had no decorations or pictures of any kind in our school inside or outside. Flowers were not allowed even in the Bermuda grass tiny yard.

I liked this schoolhouse and its location because we had much more room than in Uncle Eli's living room. We didn't have as long a walk through fences, past any mean bulls, or through muddy fields. We walked from our home east down the gravel road, across the bayou bridge and down a field lane leading to the schoolhouse. This is the schoolhouse and classroom I would attend for the rest of my school days.

It was great being in school again with my many aunts and uncles all older than myself except for Benja. He was three years younger than I. My Aunt Leah, four years older than I, shared many of the same interests with me. We managed to chat at recess about our schoolwork, Bible memory verses, and our pigeons. I taught Leah to crochet and that was a joy. I did miss visiting with Uncle David after school. There were about half the students now as in Lael Valley because the Schrock family was excommunicated, and the Amstutz family was still left behind in Lael Valley. Both were large families. I felt thankful I was not hauled off and dumped far away. I wanted to do what was right and be the best I could. I wanted peace and happiness and was willing to do anything for it.

The first week in my third year at Lael Parochial School that fall, my teacher tested me and said that I knew all she had to teach in the third grade and recommended that I skip third grade. After consulting with The Elder and my parents, they decided to put me in fourth grade. Fred stayed in third grade. I wished he could skip with me, but they didn't let him. I remember my teacher giving me many third-grade-spelling words as she tested me. I don't know why or how I knew them, but I guess I did because they told me to skip the third grade.

My third year in school I was in the fourth grade. Excited with zeal I was happy to learn all that I was given. Some new books, geography and Jewish history, were bought after the book burning. Our English books were never replaced because The Elder said that the children did not need any English. Our main history book was the Bible. The older students studied Jewish history. I learned Bible history like who was the oldest man in the Bible and what kings reigned during what time and who the prophet was at that time. I learned the major and minor prophets. It was in this grade that I learned that there was a calendar year, and I learned to write it. I even made a calendar. I learned more than reading, writing, and arithmetic that year. I always enjoyed school and the learning it brought me.

It was in the fall of 1956, during cotton-picking season, that Uncle David died. His death really hurt me. I felt like my heart sank to the soles of my bare feet, yet I was not to show any emotions. I recall having the most severe toothaches at night, and I rolled up in a ball and lay still and wide awake thinking about Uncle David. *Where is he now? He will never feel pain again. He won't be cooped up anymore like he was for more than three years.* The police involvement put a scare into the leader, the colony, and me. This changed even our school. The Elder warned that the government might close our school and terrible things might happen now that they know we exist. He told us to learn all things as fast as we could, especially the Bible.

When school started late that fall, I recall my teacher saying how hard it was for her to be taken by police to identify her brother, David. The sting of his death in our midst was hard. Yet as an eight-year-old, I tried to learn all within touch and everything my eyes saw before the government closed our school. We had instructions from The Elder as to what to do if government authorities came. Nobody was to say a word unless they asked if we have a Bible or if we believe in God. We were to answer only those two questions.

We saw how Uncle Zack was treated when he wouldn't talk after Uncle David's death, and he did as The Elder had instructed. I felt authorities might kill us if we did not talk or might destroy all our books especially the Bible. Therefore I had to learn all I could and fast. If I escaped the attack, I would have God's Word hidden in my heart and nobody could take what was there. All this put in me the fear of outside, worldly people. The Elder also warned that authorities might kill us if we say we believe in God. So I was prepared to die. If I was asked if I had a Bible, I would say, "Yes!" And if I was asked if I believe in God, I would say, "Yes!" and boom they would kill me."

Now many years later my eyes keep twitching and my liver continues to quiver as I struggle to write this chapter. I never realized all these warnings and fears affected me that much other than making me learn fast. It's been almost fifty years since that fall.

Later that year The Elder left with Uncle Eli and his family and nobody knew where they went. This was under The Elder's instructions. I missed Uncle Eli's family and often wondered where they went and how they were.

That year our colony received word that Uncle Willie Miller, Grandpa Miller's brother, was in federal prison for draft evasion. The Elder had kept him hidden because of the draft and then excommunicated him. This hurt to think of Uncle Willie locked up in a prison. *That seems much worse than Uncle David being cooped up at home,* I thought. These things gave me more to think about than schoolwork. I channeled my energy into working hard and learning fast despite my many toothaches. My teeth caused my jaws to swell. Sometimes it was one jaw and sometimes both. Sometimes my upper teeth were the cause; sometimes the lower teeth were to blame. Sometimes all four jaws were swollen and ached. Pus often drained in my mouth from big pus pockets near my teeth. This was extremely painful. I often wondered what it would be like not to hurt most of the time. I was well-trained to suffer. I had to accept the pain and learn to live with it.

When I finished my assignments, the teacher let me help my brother and sister. I enjoyed that. I drilled them on spelling words and helped them with arithmetic flash cards. I memorized all the multiplication tables fast. My teacher tried to keep me busy.

We had no music or singing of any kind. I never heard or knew anything about music. We had no sports of any kind. I had no idea what sports were or even meant. We had no table games or yard games. I did not know games existed. We had no art of any kind. I heard of drawing when somebody drew a tree and was sharply disciplined for it. The Elder had banned drawing anything, even trees. I did have an urge to draw trees and things I saw; yet I knew better than ever try or condemnation would nip me. We had no contact with the outside world. I never saw or read a newspaper or magazine. We had only a few books and all were approved by The Elder. He censored everything including the Sears Roebuck catalog. He had Ruby use an ink blotter to put long sleeves, dresses, and pants on the people in it.

I was willing to abide by all the rules to prevent the chance of being hauled off and dumped. By now it was after my day of reckoning when I had made a commitment to the Lord to do my best to be good, do only what is right, and to follow Him for the rest of my life no matter what happened. I was willing to comply with any orders and all rules.

The Elder had students make books he designed. He called them the Scripture Line books, and the El-Elohe-Israel books. The Scripture Line book contained the chapter headings of every chapter in the King James Bible. The El-Elohe-Israel book began with a nice compilation of The Elder's sayings with scriptures in the first twenty pages. The middle contained twenty-two pages of Psalm 119:1-176 divided up by the Hebrew alphabets and having eight verses under each letter. His book ended with sixteen pages of stories about Purim, Queen Esther, Mordecai and The Jews. Aunt Ruby was The Elder's main typist for his material.

At age ten I learned to type on the school's old manual Royal typewriter, but I was never allowed to type for The Elder. When I finished my assignments, I was allowed to help Ruby and Erma run the duplicator. I turned the handle and watched the papers print, fly through, and stack up. I enjoyed helping with printing. Later I learned to set type and to dual print with two colors. I liked the challenge of lining it all up, adjusting it, and printing. Seeing the finished prints was rewarding.

We began learning the Scripture Line book as we learned the Bible. I had the Scripture Line book memorized by age eleven and nobody could catch me in contests. I still have an old school Scripture Line test on chapter headings over the entire Bible with a 100% score, an A+, dated April 24, 1960. After I knew all the headings of every chapter in the Bible, I rehearsed them every week.

My teacher assigned me to learn the longest chapter in the Bible, the 176 verses of Psalm 119. I still recall the day I stood up in school and recited the entire chapter without stopping. My teacher looked surprised when I finished. Then I asked her if I could say the shortest chapter in the Bible, Psalm 117. It had only two verses and she let me. She was surprised I had learned it too. I also learned all the Hebrew alphabet and could say all the letters and write them.

We had a lot of scriptures to learn including the nine blocks as we called them. The Elder had chosen a bunch of scriptures, some chapters, and several had only verses. He placed them in nine sets of five scriptures each. My teacher struggled to find enough for me to learn and stay busy. When she gave me extra assignments, I often did them before she found more to assign. I almost felt guilty when she said, "Are you done already? I don't know if I have time to get more work for you."

I must have been somewhat of a pain for her. At that time I never realized I learned quickly. I was only trying to do what I was told and learn much before the government closed our school. I wanted to keep up with what I thought the older children were doing. I learned years later that many older students did not learn and do what I thought they did.

I learned the nine blocks of scriptures, and she had me keep going over them and writing them. She had me write Psalm 119, all the Scripture Lines — Bible chapter headings, and Bible genealogy reports. I still have much of the written material. When all we had to learn from was the Bible and a few other books, my teacher was left with very little to teach year after year.

One of my most embarrassing moments in school was the day I turned eleven when I went up in front of the school room to the card rack to write Bible verses with cards. Aunt Ruby motioned me back to her desk and told me of a fist size spot of blood on the back of my dress. My teacher understood and quickly excused me from school to go home and change clothes. I twisted the back of my long dress to my side and walked home. After changing clothes I returned to school not wanting to face anybody.

Our school years varied a lot because it was based on the weather and the cotton season. I recall a wet fall when school did not start until January. We only had about three months of school that year. Most of the time school started between October and December and ended in April. I remember a few short school years. We tried to make up a couple weeks in the summer between hoeing and picking cotton. That rarely happened because most of the time when hoeing was over picking started in another field. We were happy to get six months of school each year. Sometimes we had only three months. We never had nine months. School was not a priority. Working came first so that we had enough to eat for the year.

My urge to learn never seemed to diminish. I recall hearing Aunt Erma saying that she was going to learn the five books of Moses and that she was well on her way. I wanted to be like her. I started at the beginning of Genesis.

At age eleven I had read the Bible through once on my own and was starting through the second time. We also read the Bible in our reading class in school. After age eleven reading aloud from the Bible in school became very painful for me as I matured. Girls were not allowed to read the Bible aloud during menstrual time because we were considered unclean until completely done and a bath taken before the sun set. At that time we had to hand the teacher a note saying we could not read. This became so embarrassing for me that it severely affected my reading. I would get out of breath and stumble over words. My heart would pound so hard I felt my pulse in my face and heard it in my ears. The trauma experienced during these teen years affected me so severely that even as an adult it has been difficult to read aloud in formal settings.

I became so self conscious of all that and of my development that I joined my Aunt Leah and wore a coat all the time, summer and winter. I stayed covered. Some called the coat a shield. I felt more comfortable wearing my coat or jacket. Of course I was already dressed heavy wearing a dress, slip, and under pants below my ankles and a long sleeved blouse. Aunt Kay and I had the same problem and it hurt me to hear and see her try to read aloud. Seeing her even made my heart pound hard and I felt flush. This was painful!

I continued learning fast, and my teacher decided to have me make things in school like sewing clothes by hand. Once she had me sewing I was nonstop. I made a dress, blouse, two head coverings, slip, nightgown and two night coverings, an apron, a headscarf, a headband, and a jacket all hand stitched. I sewed my dad a shirt and crocheted my mom a sweater. I enjoyed doing that for them. I also crocheted slippers, socks, mittens, gloves, a scarf, and a doily. I made a towel, wash cloth, a dish towel, and a dish rag. I still have a list of all those things I made, but I only have Mom's worn out sweater and an old stained dish towel. I surely enjoyed sewing and crocheting all those things. We were limited to making one of each item, and I ran out of things to make.

After my mom was excommunicated school life changed, and my siblings and I were shunned. This hurt extremely deep into my soul. Nobody talked to us except the teacher. They would not even look at us. It felt like we were poison ivy and the others feared catching it from us. Of course my name was also changed from Lois to Patricia, and the pain I felt from that wound cut deep. I was ordered to remove my colony name, Lois, from all my school things and put

Patricia on them. It seemed nothing could heal this situation.

Then my dad had a mental break down. He walked off and the police picked him up, and he was institutionalized. This was the first time I felt it was hard for me to concentrate on my schoolwork. Things seemed clouded and went from bad to worse. The bitter reality of Dad's illness and hospitalization broke me inside. I decided to keep rehearsing all the Bible scriptures I had learned in order to retain them.

Once things cleared with Dad I would learn more even faster. Perhaps The Elder might lift the *bann* he placed on my family — at least on me — if my mom was the one in the red with him and God. This really concerned me. I lived with the hope of getting my good name back and being able to enjoy my aunts, uncles, and cousins again. I wanted peace at any price and no more rejection and discord in our midst.

There were even more lessons to be learned.

Patricia Hochstetler

Chapter 13

Surviving Lael Colony

The Elder was gone! One day — without explanation to anyone except Grandpa — he left the colony. There was no assurance he would return.

Everyone was perplexed and troubled. The men talked. The women talked. Even the children talked. Finally Grandpa in great distress made a moving presentation.

"I don't know how much longer we can go like this not knowing what to do without The Elder's advice. *Ick ben moot low* (I am in a low mood). Not having our Sabbath meetings doesn't help. It seems the Lord is not present. I'm afraid something terrible will happen or what's left of the colony will fall apart completely. Just remember to stay devoted to what The Elder taught even if it means death. Keep your minds stayed on the Lord as he often said. Depend on God to guide you and take care of us until His servant returns. I hope The Elder will return. He was pretty upset when he ordered me to buy him a one way bus ticket to the White House. And you never know what might happen when someone goes there. That's the government's place, wicked and of the Devil. The Elder could get killed there for his belief."

We listened to Grandpa's lecture, and remained distraught. Each person tried to learn as much of the Bible as they could while toiling in the fields. Members waited for time to pass and prayed for The Elder's return.

One day — without fanfare — The Elder came walking in. It was as if God Himself had descended from the sky and appeared in our midst. New hope shined in faces. God allowed His servant to return. What a miracle this seemed.

The Elder announced, "I went to the White House and got some things straightened out about the military. I also went to Oregon and found some people named Flory. They believe like we do, and they will be part of God's chosen one hundred forty-four thousand like you."

This gave us much courage and even more faith in The Elder and what he taught. Now we felt there were others somewhere in the world who believe just like we do. If we're good enough and obey, some day we would see them in heaven if not on earth.

"Work hard like the ants," The Elder reminded us. "The Bible refers to the ants as people. Be like ants. Protect and learn from the ants and how they lived in their colonies. See how they get along and work together."

I watched ants by the hours on the Sabbath as I recited Bible verses. The ants built little dirt crumb mounds around the entrance to their tiny home in the earth. How peaceful they seemed. They never fought, fussed, or pushed each other to stay on their busy, dirt paths. They all seemed willing to step aside unless they were busy with a heavy load. When meeting other members on their narrow, dirt paths, they always tried to help each other carry food, and they knew when not to help. They never forgot which direction they were headed. It was obvious they kept the Golden Rule. I wondered *what language do they speak, and how do they know exactly what to do and when*. They carried food in a steady stream. They gently carried their dead members out, and sometimes carefully moved eggs and babies. The ants amazed me. They did not excommunicate each other. So why did our leader and colony? *Why were we not more like the ants?* I wondered.

I also spent hours watching the spiders weaving their webs. Some spiders were colorful, some dull, but all wove with indescribable talent. My unanswered questions remained. *How can all that weaving string or web thread come out of the small creatures bottom end? Where do they store it? How do they know the distance between webs and how and where to increase or decrease the exact amount?*

Life, people, and things around me were fascinating and a challenge. I enjoyed living, learning the Bible, working, watching the birds, trees, the sky, weather and clouds.

I felt grown up as we began picking cotton the fall I was ten. Then I became very sick. It seemed much worse than the many colds, flu, and toothaches I endured each year.

I lay in bed too sick to get up. I wondered what would happen with me. I felt terribly weak, hot, and unable to eat.

Beside the head of my twin bed on my tiny, old, apple-box desk, which my father had made for me, lay an outdoor thermometer. We didn't have a thermometer for humans, and I had no idea about the harmful effects of a fever. But I felt like I was burning up, and that scorching fall day I wondered if I could reach the thermometer. After laying there looking at it and wondering for some time if I could get it, I decided to try. Using every ounce of strength I had, I reached for the thermometer. I got it. I placed my thumb and index finger on the round, red, mercury bulb. The mercury quickly shot up way above 100. I remembered Mom saying human temperature was 98.6 degrees. I wondered *what in the world is wrong with me. How can my temperature be so high above normal?*

I left the thermometer in bed where my hand had pulled it. I was too sick to return it to my desk. I dozed off. Later in the evening Mom quietly came in, and I felt her pick the thermometer up from my bed. There was a long pause before she said, "Oh, no!" and walked out of the room. Too weak to move, I felt as if I was floating in the sky and being carried by the air. Night came and went.

I heard my family in the kitchen and soon things were quiet. I believe Mom stayed home for a wash day and to stay with me. I heard her go in and out of my room but do not recall saying anything to her. That afternoon my eyes opened for a short time, and I saw the calendar hanging on the wall. The date was the twentieth.

I know this is my last day to live, I kept thinking. *Tomorrow*

*I will be dead. Then there will only be Mom, Dad, and my brother
and sister in our family. It doesn't matter. I believe I will likely be
in heaven tomorrow because I asked God to forgive me for all the
sins in my life as the Bible says to do. The Bible says God will
forgive, and I believed He did. I'm too weak to do anything evil
and I will be careful not to think anything evil before I die. I know
God knows the promise of commitment I made to Him last year
when I was nine and that was for the rest of my life even if it ends
now. I sure hope I see Grandma Miller in heaven. Oh, did I fall
asleep and not say my prayer last night? I will say it again now
to make sure.* Then a perfect, fearless peace over-shadowed
me after I lay motionless in my bed and prayed my evening
prayer in mid-day.

That evening Dad came in and sat on the side of my
bed. He spoke softly, "I went to The Elder and asked what
to do about you being sick. The Elder said maybe you or
someone in our family did wrong and God is punishing us
in this way. Did you do wrong that you know of, or do you
know of anybody in our family who did?"

I heard him, but I was too weak to move my tongue
and mouth, and I could not respond or answer him. He
continued, "The Elder said we should ask God to forgive all
of us for any sins in our lives. He said if you have enough
faith and if our family has enough faith you will live, and if
not, you will die."

I could tell Dad was stressed and stumbled for words. I
wanted to say that I knew of no sins and all would be well
without me. But I couldn't do more than think the words.
Dad prayed unlike I ever heard him pray before. It was not
the same repeated table and floor prayers given him by The
Elder which I had heard so many times. This prayer seemed
to come from Dad's heart and in earnest desperation. It was
new and different. I liked it. After praying, Dad sat silent on
the edge of my bed for awhile.

"I know you're too sick to talk, Lois, but there's nothing
more I can do," he whispered.

Then I felt him get up, and I heard his footsteps as he
left my bedroom. I wanted to call out and tell him that life

would be fine without me on earth. I wouldn't have all those terrible toothaches any more, he wouldn't have to worry about me at all, and I was happy and thankful. Even with my eyes closed things seemed extremely bright, and there seemed to be a focal point far away and things seemed small.

When I woke up later, there was nobody in my bedroom. Silence filled the air, and my ears felt plugged. The first thing I saw when my eyes opened was that calendar hanging on the wall. It dawned on me that earlier I thought I would be dead tomorrow, and I wondered what day it was.

I must have dozed off again for I heard some noise in the kitchen before I saw Mom. She peeked into my room and in a surprised voice she said, "Oh, you're awake. How do you feel?"

"Better," I responded weakly.

"Do you want anything to eat or drink?"

"No."

"I'll get you some water."

Mom returned as I stared at the calendar on the wall. "Mom, what's the date today."

"It's the twenty-third."

How can this be? I thought I would be dead tomorrow, and it's three days later now and I'm not dead. I didn't die. Why? Maybe I will live. Did I have faith? Did my family have faith? Is this a miracle? I can't believe I'm not dead.

"I'll help you drink some water," Mom insisted and lifted the glass to my lips.

I didn't want to tell her again that I didn't want anything, so I tried to sip the water. It tasted terrible! When I didn't want more, she set the glass on my desk.

"Mom, where is everybody else?"

"They're in the field working." She stood by my bed and smiled. "I made fresh bread today. Would you like some?"

"No."

"Well, I'll put a small piece on your desk where you can reach it when you feel hungry." Mom took the glass with her and left the room.

I dozed off and woke again and looking around I noticed

the thermometer. It was on my desk just like it had been earlier. *Can I reach it? I don't feel like lifting my arm to get it, but I wonder what my temperature is now.*

I forced myself to reach the thermometer. With shaky hands I grasped it, placed my thumb and index finger in place on the mercury bulb, and waited for a final reading, perhaps 98.6. I was shocked when I looked closely. My temperature was not even near 98.6! It was only in the high seventies. I don't remember the exact number, but I do know it was far below average. I wondered, *am I half-dead?* I feel cold. *Has rigor mortis set in?* Mom returned and I asked her why she thought my temperature was so low.

"I don't know or understand it at all," and she handed me a slice of fresh bread. "Why don't you try a bite of bread? It will help you gain strength."

The bread tasted better than the water, and the next sip of water tasted better than before.

"Mom, why don't I remember these last three days?"

"You must have been in a semi-conscious state or unconscious."

"What's been happening?"

"On Friday, I stayed home and washed clothes and got things ready for the Sabbath. Saturday was the Sabbath so we rested and read the Bible. Sunday I stayed home and did mending. Today, Monday, I stayed home and baked bread. Do you think you will feel like going to the field tomorrow and laying in the truck if we park it in the shade?"

"I don't know, but I don't feel like it now."

"If you eat, you might feel good enough to go," Mom urged.

The day seemed long. Evening came and the rest of my family came home from the field. They came into the bedroom to see me and were excited that I felt better. It was soon obvious that I needed more rest.

The next morning I felt even better yet very weak. My parents made a bed in the truck for me, and I went to the cotton field. They parked the truck in the shade, and I slept there most of the day. I still ate very little.

My family checked on me after each round down and back in the cotton rows. Once in the late afternoon when Mom was checking, she commented, "Your skin is turning yellow, and so are the whites of your eyes."

My skin and the whites of my eyes stayed mustard yellow for several days and then began to fade. It was a long time before I gained back my strength and felt normal. After some time I began going in the field and picking alongside family members and putting cotton in their sacks. I did not pull a cotton sack until I was stronger, and then I often lay on it and rested in the shade of tall cotton stalks. My record of pounds picked that year was not very high.

Years later I asked Mom about that illness. She responded. "I felt terribly bad knowing there was nothing I could do for you and knowing you might die. It really struck me hard when you turned yellow. I realized then how sick you actually were. I thought people turned yellow only when they had yellow jaundice and that they usually die with that."

"Mom, what do you think I had?"

"I don't know, and I guess we will never know since we weren't allowed to see doctors. I'm sure thankful you lived through it and didn't die."

"I am to. Through that experience I learned I'm not afraid to die. When the body shuts down and becomes too weak to function, the mind accepts it. Maybe I had more childlike faith than I realized."

My recovery seemed slow and the work in the fields hard yet I realized The Lord spared my life. I decided that I could now trust Him for anything and everything. Since I was having a second chance, I developed a new and deeper devotion toward God, The Elder, and the Bible.

"Mom," I said one day, "I think my life-death experience was a test of faith. I guess some things are not as important as they used to be." She nodded as I added, "This second chance makes me want to learn the Bible better."

Sickness can be a life-altering event in the life of a child, and I learned to evaluate things differently than before.

As a child, it was hard for me to understand my Dad's

mental condition. It hurt to see him suffering, and it hurt to feel the pain of what he said and did and to know he was not responsible for anything.

When I was about twelve, Dad accused me of saying and doing something at school which caused The Elder to reject a book Dad had purchased for the school library. He bought it without permission from the Elder when he was supposed to buy groceries. I had nothing to do with that book at any time. Dad sent the book to school with Fred, and Fred carried it home after The Elder rejected it. Yet Dad approached me the next day after school. He demanded, "What did you say that caused The Elder to reject my book?"

"Dad, I didn't say anything about the book to anybody."

"What did you do to cause the rejection then?" Dad shouted.

"Nothing. I didn't do anything or say anything," I pleaded.

"You're lying to me. I want you to tell me the truth about this matter. You hear me?"

"Yeah, but Dad, I didn't. . . ." I shuttered.

"You did it, and you know you did it. Now tell the truth. Come on, just say the truth."

"Dad, I am, and I don't know what more to say."

"All right, Lois, if you won't tell me the truth, you must sit on this old wooden chair until bedtime." He pointed at the most uncomfortable seat in the house.

I didn't know what to do. This was Friday afternoon, and it was time to prepare for the Sabbath. Mom reminded him that we needed to feed the animals, clean the house, and take baths — all before sundown. Then Dad sternly said, "You can get off that chair long enough to do your chores and take a bath. Then you get back on the chair."

I had a lot more to think about doing chores than I usually did. *How can this actually be happening?* After finishing my duties I returned to the old wooden chair of punishment.

"Lois, come off that chair long enough to say our floor prayer, and then you get back on it."

Dad moved the chair to the kitchen and ordered me to

sit on it instead of my usual seat at our table. After Dad read a Bible chapter and said the table prayer my family began eating. I had to watch, but I was not allowed a bite of food. Really I had no appetite by this time.

"Lois, if you can't tell the truth, you don't need to eat. Sit there! If you want food, tell the truth." Dad sharply informed me.

I've been taught not to lie and I'm not lying to get food now. I won't lie. I'll go hungry.

"Can I go to bed?" I asked.

"No," Dad replied, "not until everybody is done eating. You can go to bed then. If you aren't going to be honest, you better think all night about telling the truth in the morning."

Eventually everyone finished eating and I went to bed. Feeling puzzled, I said my bedtime prayer and lay in bed wide-awake. My stomach growled as I tried to think my way out of this situation without lying like Dad insisted I was doing. I remembered my promise to The Lord to always obey Him, my parents, and do what is right. *Now what do I do, Lord, when my Dad asks me to do wrong and lie? Is this another test of faith?* I finally dozed off only to wake a few minutes later and wonder what would happen in the morning.

Dad got up earlier that morning than he did on most Sabbath mornings. We ate breakfast, and then Dad asked, "Lois, have you decided to tell me the truth yet?"

"Yes, and it is the same as before," I choked out. "I didn't say or have anything to do with The Elder not allowing that book in the school library."

"If that's the way you are going to be, you sit here in this chair in the middle of the living room and face me." Dad ordered, and I sat. "Now confess what you said and did or you will be sitting here all day."

I would not confess all morning under this tension as Dad talked to himself and to his spirit friends. At noon Dad said, "You are the most bullheaded, stubborn child. Get off that chair, and we'll have dinner."

"Dad, can I go to the toilet?" I asked.

"Go and hurry back inside. It's dinner time and I can't

believe you're so stubborn."

After the floor prayer — Dad obviously upset with me — said, "You sit right back in that chair until you decide to admit that you're lying. Be honest!"

I knew better than to say anything, and I had no appetite. I waited quietly as the sun crept across the sky. Everyone finished eating that noon and Dad looked at me with glaring disapproval and said, "Now if you aren't going to confess, you are sitting in our jail for the bad. I want a nap."

Our jail was in the hall beside Dad's bedroom. It was a place I tried hard to stay out of. It was a four by four room made by opening two doors toward a corner and hooking them together. In the jail was a five gallon metal can full of tallow for our seat. There I sat all afternoon until sunset. Dad — still upset with me — said, "You are bullheaded and strong willed. Now come out of jail for supper."

Dad let me sit at the table this time. I ate very little and then went to bed early. The next day I asked Mom, "Why do you think Dad did that to me when I didn't do or say anything in school about his book?"

"The Elder rejected the book, and if you didn't say or do anything, you did the right thing by not lying."

Mom's support felt good, but Dad would not talk to me for weeks after that. Hurting inside I continued trying to do what was right to please both my dad and The Elder.

In obedience to Dad we all lined up and waited for Christ's return or sunrise. When the sun rose in a few very tense moments and Christ never returned, Dad dismissed us to do chores and we were late getting to the field without breakfast.

One day during hoeing season Dad was having problems. On his orders we left the field at noon. He insisted we run rapidly out of the field. He was shouting, "Something is going to get us, and the end of the world is coming. Follow me! Follow me!"

He led us through brush and briers. Once he walked over a large snake. We witnessed him nearly stepping on the snake and urged him to be careful, but I doubt he even heard us. Fred quickly killed the snake as we were commanded to, and we went on.

We struggled to keep up with Dad. Once we reached the truck and almost before we were in and the doors shut, he sped off. Halfway home he suddenly pulled off to the side of the road, jumped out, and ran into a big brier patch. He stood there for several hours as we waited in the truck. He finally returned with many brier scratches, and we went home that afternoon without pay.

These were some days to remember. It took a big mixture of patience, tolerance, and sympathy for our Dad, and trust in God to survive in Lael Colony.

How could it get any worse?

Patricia Hochstetler

Chapter 14

Shunned

"Mom, what happened at the schoolhouse in that special meeting?" I asked many years later.

"I was assumed guilty and nothing I said made any difference. The question there was not if I was guilty. The question was would I confess to how much money I had. I tried to say I didn't have any money. I was ignored and the issue of me confessing was the only alternative. I saw it did no good for me to open my mouth. My father said if I wasn't going to confess, they might as well go home."

Mom sat quietly as she relived that moment. She struggled to regain her composure.

"Everybody sat silent for a while, and then I was told to leave. That's when I tried to go home, and my legs wouldn't hold me up after I went out the back door. I collapsed on the ground. I felt like I wanted to die there rather than go to hell later."

Mom's eyes were moist when she continued. "Nobody will ever know how painful that was for me. Then as I sat in the yard behind the schoolhouse my father came out the door, saw me, and said, 'You mean you're still here?'

"I felt as though I was the scum of the earth, left to the Devil, and waiting for eternal hell. That's when I decided I was not sitting on their ground any longer! I would not stay in their way even if I had to crawl all the way home on my hands and knees. I crawled a bit, and then tried again and rose to my feet. I could barely walk home. I was doomed to hell by The Elder. Then he ordered the colony to use a *meiding* on me and all of our family."

I was about to discover how cruel a *meiding* could be.

The colony people quit talking to our family. They ignored us as if we were non-existent. In the cotton fields they purposely started at the other end of the field every morning. Whenever we appproached workers — relatives — in the rows of the cotton field, we were ignored and avoided even when it was inconvenient for them.

Their feelings appeared as flat as the Delta land, and their outlook as dark as the stormiest cloud I had ever seen. No flicker of emotions showed on their faces. Their actions spoke loud and clear. When we came to the middle of the field and passed them going in opposite directions, the ones bordering our rows left their rows and helped other until we passed the spot where they were working. These actions showed they did not even want to get near us as if we were contaminated or poisonous. This was their *meiding* on us, and of course they would not eat with us.

Deception, distrust, and disunity were destroying our colony. The Elder's unsubstantiated accusation of my mom was the cause. Pain was not hers alone! Dad suffered. Fred suffered. Joan suffered. I suffered. And so did all the members of Lael Colony! There was no turning back now. The Elder had charted a course, and the damage followed. It was now even beyond his control.

Decades later I asked Mom about this matter.

"I felt extremely bad to see you children shunned by everybody, even your grandfather and my brothers and sisters. It hurt me terribly for my dad to believe that I was doomed to hell because The Elder declared it. I was crushed when he used such a tough *meiding* on me. He wouldn't even get within eight feet of me while working in the field. He treated me like I was evil enough to be the Devil himself. Yet I knew *that he knew* I didn't do what I was accused of. Why didn't he tell me that he knew it?

"They all sealed their lips and said nothing. Such fear! Such deception! This severe kind of shunning hurt me to the core of my entire being. I didn't know what to do or if there was anything I could do." Mom choked up and tears filled her eyes. "I did the best I knew to cope. It still hurts to think about it after more than forty years. I lost all those years . . . lost my family . . . because of an accusation that was not even true. I was brainwashed almost to the point that I felt insane."

"Mom, how did you cope with it?"

"I thought of my mother and what she told me about how she dealt with her emotional upheaval when The Elder accused her of the lack of respect for her husband. 'That man of God turned my own children against me,' she said. My mother was distraught, but life had to go on.

"Your grandmother grieved all she could, and she finally came to the realization that God knows all. She was determined to do her best to please Him. I decided to follow my mother because she was so level-headed. Knowing her strength helped me even after she was gone," Mom concluded.

In spite of Mom's excommunication, The Elder gave us permission to attend Lael Parochial School. Although we could sit in class, we were not allowed to talk to anybody except our teacher. The other children could not talk to us. This hurt!

This is about the same time The Elder decided to change my name again. He took away my Bible name, Lois, which he had given me at the age of four, and changed it back to my worldly birth name, Patricia. *Why? He never told me why. Wasn't I good enough for my Bible name anymore? Since I lost my Bible name, would I be doomed to hell like Mom? Was this a part of shunning?*

School was extremely hard for three weeks that summer between hoeing and picking cotton. This was also an especially hard time with Dad under the pressure of his mental state and Mom's excommunication. There was the added stress when The Elder predicted the end of the world which didn't happen.

No one was prepared for that shocking morning a few days later when Grandpa brought the news, "The Elder is gone! He's disappeared. I can't find any trace of him. What are we going to do now?" This news spread rapidly among the colony fathers even though by this time The Elder had almost completely isolated each family. "What did we do wrong?" Grandpa kept asking.

Shunning is a terribly humiliating experience. Unable to communicate with outsiders might be understandable, but the inability to fellowship with your own extended family is both cruel and destructive.

Meanwhile my brother, Fred, could not cope with our family situation. The shunning was affecting him more than any of us could realize. His forced separation from Besodiah, his uncle and only real friend was intolerable. Besodiah, who was actually eight months younger than Fred, found it equally difficult. At the age of fourteen they felt the need to make some choices.

One morning Fred saw Besodiah approaching along the row in the cotton field. In spite of the danger it was worth the risk! Eye contact was friendly. No one was too close. Fred whispered, "We've gotta meet." Besodiah only nodded. Those three words spoke volumes. They skillfully timed the cotton picking so they met in the next row. "Tonight at 9:00." That was the only comment. Friends know where to meet friends.

That night was the start of secret meetings. They met and discussed the pain of our families' crisis and the colony situation and plotted their escape. After a few months of continuing to meet secretly at night, they ran away.

The next morning when Mom discovered Fred was not is his room she quickly told Dad.

His response was immediate. He dashed out the door and headed for Grandpa's. Neither man was surprised to learn that both boys were gone. They stepped away from the house and beyond hearing distance. Only fathers could talk to each other. After deciding a course of action, Dad and Grandpa returned to their families and shared the news that both boys were gone.

We went to the field and picked cotton, and the news created a stir and scare in the colony. Everyone's thoughts focused on the two, young, strayed, missing sinners. What will happen? Is this another situation like David's? Will the authorities get involved?

I felt sick inside to think Fred was missing. *My brother, my friend and work companion was gone! Would it be like Uncle David's case, and we would never see them alive again? They know nothing of the world or how to exist outside our colony. What will happen to them?*

After all Mom had been through, it didn't seem fair to see her under this kind of distress. It hurt so bad she could hardly take it. "One of the cruelest things a child can do to their parents is to run away and leave their parents not knowing what happened," she said.

That's exactly what happened to Grandma Long when my dad and mom left and took us, her three grandchildren. My great grandparents, Dan and Nancy Miller, lost seven of their eleven children and many grandchildren when they all disappeared with The Elder.

Nobody reported Fred and Besodiah missing. We knew The Elder's advice would be don't tell anyone and don't involve the law. We waited long stressful days. We feared the boys would starve in the woods or somewhere. One evening in the kitchen we noticed something different with the can opener, and it appeared that somebody had been there while we were gone. Was this good news or bad news? A couple of days later it seemed some canned jars of food had been moved.

Taking notice of this, we began to set things so we could see if they were moved. We wondered if the boys might have come to our house during the day while we were in the field. Sure enough, it became obvious someone was sneaking in and getting food. We assumed it was the boys, and it felt good to believe at least one of them was alive. Mom wanted to stay home and watch and wait for them, but Dad said no. *How could we know it was Fred and Besodiah? Could we see them and talk to them? We hoped they were the intruders.*

According to Dad, Grandpa's family also became suspicious that somebody was sneaking into their shed of stored canned food at night while they said prayers, read the Bible, and ate. Grandpa set the trap by praying and reading a bit earlier than usual. Then he sat quietly in the shed while the rest of his family went on as usual sitting and pretending to be going through their usual routine.

Besodiah came after dark. Grandpa caught him in the act of taking food. Grandpa was upset yet relieved. He made Besodiah stay there by the shed. He called the other ten family members outside. Zack was ordered to get a good size switch to punish Besodiah. He pulled a knife from his pocket and cut what he saw as a large switch. Grandpa didn't accept it and told Zack to get a larger one. He did. Grandpa kept ordering a larger one until the switch was thumb size. Then he ordered all the brothers and sisters to witness Besodiah's punishment.

Years later I asked Besodiah what happened that day.

"I got caught getting food to survive," Besodiah answered. "Then I was beaten in front of all my brothers and sisters. It was humiliating. I was so weak I decided to surrender to anything even if it was death. I really thought I might die. Father beat me from my neck to my heels. It hurt but I couldn't resist. I couldn't sit for a long time because of welts on my back, bottom, and legs. Father forced me to tell if I knew where Fred was. I told him."

"How did you feel after you ran away?" I asked

"At first I thought it was great. But I got scared when we walked half way to town that dark night. We slept in a cornfield. I wondered what was going to happen. I knew nothing of the outside world and wondered if we could survive in it."

Besodiah's punishment was done in obedience to The Elder's extreme emphasis about sparing the rod. This cruel punishment was done in the name of God.

Such deception!

Grandpa came and told my dad that Fred was alive and living in the woods. He expressed his concern about Fred harming himself because of being hungry, alone, and desperate.

Shunned

Dad in his mental state became angry and still would not let Mom stay home to watch for Fred. He wanted to be the first to talk to him.

I had great fear, yet I still had some hope and faith that maybe Fred would come back alive. I went to bed wondering how hungry Fred was and if he would really make it. I wished I could see him and talk him into coming home. Fred was all I thought about. He was all I wanted to talk about. I wanted Fred home. I missed him very much.

One day we were rained out of the field and went home. As we sat in our living room, we saw Fred dash from the bayou to an old vacant barn west of our house. Dad rose in anger. He grabbed a leather belt and headed for the bayou. He ordered us to stay home. He marched from the bayou to the south side of the old barn and waited. If Fred ran out the other side, he would be in an open field or on the gravel road. Dad thought he could out run Fred.

We only watched the barn and wondered what would happen inside.

Then we saw Fred come slowly out of the barn with Dad behind him ready to strike. I was glad Fred was coming home, but I felt sick at the way he looked — skinny, dirty, wet, beaten, and weak. I felt scared for him and afraid of what Dad might do next.

When he stumbled into the house, I told him I was glad he was home. I could see he was in pain, weak, and tired. He lay down listless on our wooden couch bench. He would not talk. My one day in our home-made jail was a mild punishment compared to Fred's beating. I had felt Dad's anger before and after my jail time. Fred was getting it now, and we all feared for him.

The next morning we were up early doing chores, and I talked to Fred before we went to the field. He told me of his beating, how hungry he got staying in the woods, and how they tried to catch some fish and cook them on a fire in the woods.

At least The Elder was still gone and couldn't order anybody hauled off or put a curse on us. I still feared what might happen to Fred since Dad's anger spiraled out of control at times.

Years later I asked Fred what really happened in the barn on that rainy day. He groaned. "I knew I was in for trouble when I heard Dad's voice. I started to run, but I knew I better not. I was too weak to resist. Dad grabbed me with his superior strength. He began lashing me with his wide leather belt. I truly thought he would kill me, but I was too weak to care. With each of his beating strokes I thought dying this way wouldn't be any worse than starving. I gave up on living at that point. When Dad's belt broke in two, he used the two pieces on me, and then he decided to take off the belt he was wearing and used it on me until he was too worn out to hit anymore. He told me to get up and go home. I felt like I couldn't walk, but I was not telling him."

Fed had more to share about his aborted plans to leave the colony with Besodiah. "We really wanted out of the colony. We were actually planning to walk to Colorado. Somewhere we saw a picture from there and it was beautiful. We had no idea what we were headed for. The first night it was moon lit and we walked to just north of Round A Way. Then it clouded over and got very dark. We stopped and slept in a field and got too cold to sleep. We partially buried ourselves in the dirt to stay warm until daylight. We were halfway to Clarksdale, Mississippi.

"It seemed harder when people could see us. We arrived in Clarksdale hungry. We walked to a gas station looking for a map to go to Colorado. When we came out of the station, a policeman was there and asked us what we were doing and where we were going. That scared us. We bought something to eat by taking some of the forbidden money out of those homemade money belts that The Elder had our fathers sew up tight and strap on each of the children.

"When the police left we started walking back home. It got dark going toward home and we spent another night in a field. I knew by then that we didn't know anything about the world and how to make it out there. But I didn't want to go back into the colony. Once we were in our area I was afraid to go home. I didn't know what would happen. When I got weak enough and Besodiah was caught, I kind of gave up. I felt I wouldn't go back home, but if I got caught, I wasn't resisting.

"It hurt me terribly bad when I was caught, but there was relief in it also. I knew then when I turned eighteen I would find a way out of there somehow. It was a matter of waiting the time out and not causing a disturbance. I didn't feel like complying anymore with rules, and I stayed in the shed. I snuck out and bought a radio and listened to it. Besodiah and I met in the woods at night after supper when we were supposed to be in bed. We listened to my secret tiny radio for an hour; that was until I got caught and my radio was smashed. Remember the hole I had carved in the post by my door there in the shed? That's where I hid my radio."

"I remember."

This was a painful period in our lives.

How long could we keep going on like this?

Patricia Hochstetler

Chapter 15

Forced from the Colony

Dad seemed angry most of the time and his eyes glared. We knew his extreme strength and super power when he had that strange look in his eyes. He often stood staring and did things with much force. We knew to stay out of his way whenever possible.

One day Dad said, "It won't be long now. The end of the world is coming soon. We'll all die."

Should we believe, ignore, or just go along with Dad? There was no easy choice for us. In Lael Colony every father controlled his family, and no one in the family dared show any resistance. If they did, trouble trapped them. We feared for our lives because of Dad's unpredictable behavior. Consequently we made detailed plans for escape if something drastic did happen. In that event we would meet in the bayou across the road in front of our house. We knew the exact spot to meet by a big tree.

Because he was one of Dad's main targets, Fred's nervous twitch in his face and eyes, which started at age eleven, continually worsened. Using cardboard, Fred created a room, an escape. He partitioned off a small section in the shed attached to the chicken house for his space. It was just wide enough for his bed and apple-box desk. There was a window in the small area which would be a means of escape if Dad came to his door. He came into the house only at mealtime and when Dad was gone.

Fred still talked to me some about his feelings yet he seemed quieter after he had run away. He slowly gained weight but still looked extremely thin. Meal time was not a pleasant occasion. To avoid looking at Dad during Bible reading and while eating, Fred shielded his eyes with his left hand. As soon as he finished eating, he would shade his eyes with both hands and wait quietly for everyone to finish. The problem of Dad staring at him at the table remained, and it hurt me to see it as I sat beside Fred every meal. I wanted to help him, but I couldn't. I wanted Dad to feel better. I felt helpless and fearful of what could happen if I tried. I remained quiet, did my chores, and helped all those I could. I tried to avoid any conflict and anger.

It was hard for me to sleep well at night. Dad frequently paced from one end of our shotgun house to the other talking to himself, sometimes most of the night. The wall to my bedroom was only a curtain, and each time he passed fear gripped me. Often during summer months the curtain was open leaving half of my bed exposed to the hallway.

Suddenly one night Dad sat very still on the side of my bed and put his hands on my neck. He whispered, "Tish, wake up! Wake up!"

Dad paused. His hands clamped around my neck. I froze in place without a flinch. Fearing the worst, I broke into a sweat. I held perfectly still as if already dead while Dad continued whispering to himself. Thoughts flooded my mind. *Do I rip loose and try to run? Do I lie still until his grip tightens or loosens? What should I do?*

Minutes passed. I could not understand what Dad was whispering. Terror ripped up and down my body. My head felt like exploding by the time Dad again whispered, "Tish, wake up! Wake up!" He shook me by my neck and then my shoulders. "Tish wake up and get up now! The end of the world is coming!"

Compliance was my best option. I softly answered, "Okay!" Dad withdrew his hands, and I jumped out of bed.

He went to Mom's bed across the room. Since The Elder's rule that there was to be no relations between husband and wife, my parents no longer slept together.

"Mary, wake up!" Dad shouted. "The end of the world is coming. Get up now."

Forced from the Colony

Dad hurried to Joan's bed nearby and hollered even louder, "Joan, wake up! Get up now! Right now! The end of the world is coming."

Dad left our room, and we knew he would go to the shed to awaken Fred. I feared what he would do to Fred and how it would scare him. While quickly dressing, we decided to stay in the house to see what Dad would do to him.

As we dressed, Dad raged out the back door. We knew where he was headed, and we listened fearfully. We heard Dad knocking on Fred's tiny locked door. Then we heard him holler, "Fred, Fred, wake up! Get up! The end of the world is coming."

Fred, hearing Dad at his door, jumped out of bed and bailed out through the window. He ran toward the bayou as Dad continued banging and pushing on his door until the door popped open. No Fred!

Dad turned toward the house frustrated, but he saw the light from Fred's flashlight heading to the bayou. He chased him down and brought him to the house. Then he ordered all of us out of the house and insisted we line up in front of our porch. It was midnight and we waited.

"We'll all die," Dad declared. "The end of the world is coming soon. We'll all die before sunrise."

We waited uncertain if we would die at his hand or live to escape the threatened doom. To the left of us in our dirt drive Dad paced around in circles staring at the ground and talking to himself. Shag followed him as if he knew something was going wrong. Still frightened, Fred slipped away to the bayou without Dad noticing.

Toward morning in clouded moonlight Mom, Joan and I sat on the front edge of the porch exhausted, hostage to fear and who knows what else. From the bayou, up along the fence row and behind our barn and chicken house, Fred having second thoughts chose to check on our safety and advanced to the west side of our porch.

He peeked under the wash basin shelf and whispered to Mom, "Is it safe?"

"We hope so!" Mom whispered. "It seems like Dad has really lost it this time! He thinks the end of the world is coming before the sun rises and has ordered us to stay out here and wait."

Fred started to move away.

"Fred, stay here with us," Mom pleaded.

He sat down on the porch beside us without Dad noticing him at the moment. We were all tired and knew we dare not leave. Some of us lay back on the porch with feet dangling over the edge. Suddenly Dad rushed over in front of us. "Stand up in a line ready to die," he ordered.

Dad was so spaced out that he never noticed Fred with us. Drenched in fear we all rose to our feet. *What will he do next? He's so sure we will die. Will he kill us? How can we know?*

"Should we run to the bayou when he turns his back or all escape into the soybean field?" Fred whispered.

"I want us to all stay together," Mom replied outwardly calm but inwardly in turmoil. "Let's wait it out a bit longer and see if he looks violent. He can outrun and overpower any of us."

I wanted to vanish into thin air. Yet I felt whether it resulted in life or death I must stay with my family. Just before daybreak some of us dozed off briefly but not all at the same time. By agreement one person was to constantly keep a close eye on the situation. We took turns.

As morning dawned, Dad became more intense and focused on the eastern sky as he wandered farther east. He warned us, "It's only a few more minutes. It's almost over. The end is almost here." Dad stood quietly and stared into space as Shag circled him and looked up at him. We watched and waited.

The sky lightened and soon the sun peeked over the horizon. Dad stared and stared. Slowly he walked toward us and in a low, dejected tone said, "Get ready to go to the field."

We had survived the ordeal!

Tired and weary we rushed to do our chores. Fred sharpened hoes. Joan pumped a keg of water. I fed the chickens and pigeons. Mom packed lunches and put some leftover biscuits in a bag for breakfast on the way to the field. She threw Shag a biscuit before hurrying to the field for a twelve-hour day. We were late.

This day seemed long for we were too tried to work as if nothing had happened. We worked later into the evening to make up our time. Dad lagged behind all day. We helped him hoe to enable him to catch up at the end of each row before we started another set of rows. We struggled for the rest of that hoeing season, unsure of what would happen next.

Some evenings we would bow down on our kitchen floor to pray and Dad would talk to himself or remain quiet for long periods of time before praying. We waited. Sometimes at the table he sat whispering instead of reading the Bible or saying the table prayer. We waited.

In the field we felt that horrible sting of total shunning from my grandpa, aunts, and uncles. We were cut off from our people and didn't really know what we had done. We were the nobodies struggling hard to make a living.

One day rain came and chased us out of the field. Once home the rain quit, but it was too wet to return to the field. Dad paced the house and then went outside. We knew he was in bad shape. He began walking east on our gravel road, and we watched him knowing there was nothing we could say or do to help him. Dad stopped on the road in front of Grandpa's house and stood in the middle of the road, hands down by his sides. He stood like that for fifteen to twenty minutes. Then I saw him fall straight backwards as stiff as a board. He hit his head hard on the road.

Dad lay in the road like dead.

"Oh, I wonder if that killed him?" I groaned.

Fred didn't wait for Mom to say anything but ran to see if Dad was injured. But he knew in Dad's condition it wasn't safe to get too close.

We waited. It seemed a long time before he began to move, but finally Dad sat up. He looked around as if dazed and just continued sitting in the road.

"He's alive!" Mom and I said at the same time. There was both release and fear.

"Why doesn't he get up? What if a vehicle comes?" I asked without expecting an answer. Of course there was not much traffic.

Fred, already halfway to where Dad was still sitting, noticed that Dad was looking around. He became afraid and jumped into the ditch along the road and just watched him. Dad stood up and began walking east again, and Fred fearfully followed along in the ditch. They walked out of our sight, and we could only pray that nothing serious would happen. We waited and waited. The waiting seemed endless.

Fred returned home that evening exhausted.

"I stayed in the ditch so Dad couldn't see me, and I followed him halfway to Dublin. The police came and surrounded him, so I went up there thinking it might be safe. The officer tried to talk Dad into sitting in the police car, but he wouldn't. He wasn't about to be persuaded. They ordered him to get into their car, but he still resisted when they tried to shove him into the back. Dad fought with all the strength he had. He grabbed the roof of their car and braced himself. He was not going into the back of their car! They took hold of his arms and legs and forced him onto the back seat," Fred said wide-eyed. "It took four policemen to overpower him. They said Dad was as strong as an ox. I hated to see this happening, but there was nothing I could do. They said they would get help for Dad, and then they drove off with him."

Someone on that road must have seen Dad and Fred and thought something looked strange and called the police. This experience was unpleasant, but it was safer this way. The police came back and said they put Dad in jail and would later transport him to a state mental hospital where he would get help.

Meanwhile our lives seemed much different without Dad. We picked cotton that fall, and Fred drove Dad's truck on the field roads. My crushed finger hurt a lot and I couldn't pick cotton as well and often my teeth ached. Mom weighed our cotton sacks and didn't have the strength to hang them on the scales like Dad or to push them up on the wagon to help as Fred pulled them up. We weighed our cotton sacks more often so they wouldn't be so heavy. We endured the harsh shunning from the colony, not a word said to us in the fields.

The Elder had left the colony with orders that we could still attend Lael Parochial School. Everybody must obey the rules and the shunning would remain that way until he released it. We had nobody to ask for advice or help. We were on our own!

The first frost came that fall and the smell of death on the cotton stalks filled the air when the sun rose. The stalks shriveled and died within the next few days. Our spirits also shriveled yet hope remained deep inside. We had no way to communicate with Dad. The Elder always insisted that all the families must be without any addresses or mailboxes. We waited and waited hoping we would learn something. One day Allen, the plantation manager, came and said he heard that Dad had been taken to the state mental hospital in Whitfield, Mississippi, where they had started electrical shock treatment.

We knew nothing about any treatment and could only hope and pray for God's will and protection. We finished the cotton-picking season and started school that fall. It felt good to be in the presence of the other students yet it hurt not to be able to talk to them. At least I could talk to the teacher and see the others and that helped. It was difficult for me to concentrate on my schoolwork. That was the first time I had experienced that. My mind kept wondering about what happened to Dad and how things would turn out for him.

Fred's face and eye twitches greatly improved, but he still had nightmares that Dad would be after him to kill him. I had dreams that Mom was burning in hell. I wanted to help her. There was nothing I could do, not even a drop of water on her tongue. That really hurt, and I wondered *Is Mom going to hell?* We had a lot of hard work to keep up with all the firewood, chores, working in the field, and then school.

Dad was released from the state mental hospital before school ended that spring. It felt good to have Dad home, and he seemed better. It was not long before things once more began to tense up. Fred stayed in the shed most of the time, and his face twitches returned.

Dad helped hoe cotton, but he continually lagged behind. The same old routine of talking to himself returned. He seemed to have even more anger. Or was it less control? One day as Dad told me how to do something he wanted done, I followed and listened to him. He thrust the door shut on me catching my heel in the bottom of the door which took out a big deep gash just below the ankle bone. This hurt my feelings as much as my foot. The gash became infected and required a long time to heal.

Dad angrily threatened the plantation manager later that summer. We learned about it when the police pulled up in our drive. Dad went out and they arrested him. Again Dad was taken to jail and later transported to the state mental hospital.

Once more we picked cotton without Dad. The shunning felt strong yet I sensed a weakness after attending school the past winter. Naomi, our teacher, tried hard to encourage us to do our best. This was the year she had me do a lot of sewing.

I felt I could enjoy living around my aunts and grandpa even if they had to use shunning. I knew it was not really aimed at me. I was only caught in the crossfire between The Elder and my mom's excommunication. The shunning was a gray area for my aunts and uncles because I had not done anything wrong as far as they were concerned.

It felt like we were only half a family while Dad was gone. We adjusted easier this time although his absence remained heavy on our minds. Dad had been gone a long time, and it was still difficult to cut firewood, get it out of the woods and to our home, and then cut it up for the stoves.

One day the plantation manager came to our house and

talked to Fred. "It seems to me that you folks don't have much firewood."

Fred was speechless. It was hard to admit we really needed help.

"I'll take care of it," the manager announced. Before long we found out that he said something to my grandpa about helping us. That's when he learned what shunning really means. He was amazed that Grandpa wouldn't help his own children because of the shunning The Elder had placed on us.

"Benjamin Miller, I'm ordering your boys to work for me," he announced gruffly. He turned to my uncles and said, "Go to the woods and cut a couple of wagon loads of firewood for the winter. Take it over to Clarence's family. This nonsense has to stop!"

Zack and Besodiah filled the work order. It seemed hard for them to bite and seal their lips as commanded by The Elder. It was obvious Fred and Besodiah still wanted to be friends but couldn't.

Another day the plantation manger came to our house with more news. "Clarence will be transferred from the state mental hospital to the veteran's hospital in Biloxi, Mississippi," Allen said seriously. "I want you to know that I told them that Clarence is not allowed on this plantation again if he's ever released. He threatened me, and I can't take that chance on my safety."

What would happen if they released Dad? Where would he go? We had no answers.

Somehow Dad had received word that he would not be allowed to return to the plantation. For the first time in twelve years he wrote to his mom, Bertha Long, in Elkhart, Indiana. He told her where he was and where we were. Unknown to us he had communicated with her.

Mom soon received a letter from Dad explaining what he had done. A few days later Grandma Long and Uncle Carl, Dad's brother, showed up at our home. They had come to take us back to Indiana.

"Children, you must listen and do whatever Grandma

Long tells you to do," Mom said sincerely.

I was in a quandary. I thought, *Grandma Long was declared a heathen and not fit to be around. Why are we forced to go with her now? Why must we do whatever she tells us to do? What if she tells us to do wrong?*

When Grandma Long showed up at our home, she was definitely ready to take us away. *This doesn't feel right,* I kept thinking. *They are like strangers.*

Grandma told us to stand so she could take our picture. *Listen to Mom and do whatever Grandma Long tells you,* raced through my mind. I stood there feeling very apprehensive when she took a picture of us three children.

I didn't know it, but Fred was ready to go. He had lived for this day and opportunity. I had not thought that way yet. Although things were hard, leaving did not seem like the right option for me. It didn't take long for them to help us pack everything we could in Dad's old truck and Uncle Carl's copper colored, 57 Chevy, station wagon with a white top. We loaded everything that night ready to leave early in the morning.

After breakfast, Mom, Joan, and I piled into Uncle Carl's 'loaded to the roof' station wagon with boxes stacked on the back seat between Joan and me. There was enough room for Shag on the floor near my feet; he stood wagging his tail knowing something strange was happening. *Was he saying good-bye or please take me too?*

Grandma and Uncle Carl saw Shag resting his chin on the car seat beside us and agreed to let him come along. One signal and Shag jumped in and lay down. Grandma Long drove Uncle Carl's car. Fred hopped in Dad's truck with Uncle Carl behind the steering wheel. I couldn't believe that this was really happening. It couldn't be real or right. *How could it? The world is wicked and filled with heathens. And now we were getting forced out into that world.*

We left our home before daylight. As our caravan passed Grandpa's home, a flashlight blinked in their front window. I learned later that those light flashes were deliberate to show their concern for us on that dark, dark morning. They expressed their fears that their flashlight did not give much light to help. I knew then that they dreaded to see us leave. They also seemed crippled without their leader.

As we drove down our gravel road for the last time, we passed some of the cotton fields and the only world I had known. *What will happen to Grandpa, my aunts, uncles, cousins, and all those we left behind in the colony? What will become of our home, furniture, and most of our personal belongings?*

We were each allowed to take one box of our personal things. Setting beside me, my one box contained my personal clothes and precious things like my Bible, Scripture Line book, and El-Elohe-Israel books. It also held some of my school papers and my small cedar chest with precious things like my tiny knife, chocolate meteor rock, and arrowheads. I took most of the things from my little apple box desk, but my desk had to stay behind.

Suddenly we were flying down a big, two lane, paved highway and fear wrenched me. Grandma struggled to keep up with Uncle Carl and his heavy foot on the accelerator of Dad's old truck which seldom had traveled more than 35 mph. She signaled for him to slow down, but he kept speeding down the highway at 65 miles per hour. *What kept all the cars and trucks from crashing into each other,* I wondered. I knew nothing of any rules on the road. Our dirt and gravel roads had no names or stop signs and very few vehicles and drivers. I felt so fear-stricken a knot stayed in my throat and stomach. My thoughts kept flashing back to all the dogs, cats, chickens, and pigeons we fed that morning and left behind. *Will they all starve? Why is all this happening and I have no choice in anything?* My heart had a helpless, sinking feeling.

Around mid-morning Uncle Carl stopped for gas.

"Children, I want you to go into the building and use the toilet," Mom said.

"What's a toilet," I asked.

"It's the like the outhouse but only inside."

When I saw what a real bathroom looked like, I was shocked.

"That thing there is like our basin. It's a place to wash

your hands, and it has water hooked up to it," Mom explained as she showed us how to use a faucet.

There was an even greater surprise! There was a white, shiny, stool like thing. It was different from the wooden stool I knew. This stool with a hole in the center had water swirling round and round making the deposit disappear. It didn't stink and there were no blow flies and maggots. The soft nicely rolled up toilet paper was unlike our old catalogs or corncobs. This fancy toilet place seemed nothing like our outhouse or thunder mug that sat in the corner of our closet for times when we were too sick to use the outhouse. They called that little room at the gas station a restroom. It amazed me. We all used it and popped back in the vehicles as soon as possible.

After several more hours of travel, Uncle Carl decided he would stop early for lunch.

Mom had strict instructions for us. "Children, we're going into the restaurant despite the biscuits we brought to eat. I know you've been taught that any food out in the *world* is unclean, but we have to do what Grandma says." Then in a whisper she added, "You don't have to eat anything."

This strange world was overwhelming. We didn't eat pork or use lard because of the dietary laws. I was sure they used that in the restaurant. I was not hungry at all. The knots in my throat and stomach felt larger and tighter. We filed into the restaurant, my first one to visit. People stared at us as though we were freaks from outer space. I knew our long dresses were different, yet I never thought that people would look at us like they did. I wanted to hide but couldn't.

The people with things dangling from their ears and bright red lips looked strange to me. Everything seemed so strange, and the people were hard to understand. Once we were seated I focused on a baby girl, possibly a year old, sitting in a high chair not far from us. She looked like a real doll baby to me, and I liked watching her. This was the closest look at a real baby I had ever had.

I never ate a bite of food and prayed silently. I overheard someone say the date was June 10, and I realized it was my birthday. I was sixteen years old that day. I dared not say a word to anyone, and nobody said a word about it to me.

We left the restaurant and Grandma pleaded with Uncle Carl not to travel so fast, but he still flew. Suddenly the truck stopped in the middle of the road as the transmission went out of Dad's truck somewhere there in Tennessee. Some of us stayed with the truck while Uncle Carl left in his car to get a tow truck. A wrecker service towed Dad's truck to a gas station with a service shop. We spent the night in the two vehicles. In the morning Uncle Carl and Grandma rented a small, orange, moving trailer. We unloaded our stuff off Dad's truck and into the trailer and took some things out of the station wagon so we could all fit in the car, three in the front seat and three in the back. We were forced to abandon Dad's truck.

Grandma Long and Uncle Carl worked hard to help transport us, and we appreciated their concerns. But Grandma struggled to keep Uncle Carl from tipping the hidden bottle he kept under his car seat.

Hel drove his car pulling the trailer. Both were stuffed to the maximum. He sped down the super highways at 70 mph. I felt so fear-stricken the knots stayed in my throat and stomach the entire time.

Because of his impatience, Uncle Carl passed a semi on a hill as another semi came head-on to meet us. We were sandwiched on the centerline, paralyzed in dead silence, while both semis looked as if they would touch our windows. They hugged the shoulders of the two-lane road with its steep valleys on the sides. The silence of death filled the air as darkness came over us. Sandwiched between the semis, I could feel the car shimmying, shaking, and twisting with the raging sound of wind. It felt like we were in a tornado being jostled around. In seconds light suddenly appeared and the semis were gone. We were still alive. Shaken up, Uncle Carl pulled off to the side of the road to catch his breath.

"I thought we were all going to die," Uncle Carl said with a blank, pale expression. "I need to step out of the car for awhile." His shaking knees barely held him, and he sat back down in the car. "In a few minutes I'll drive to the next restaurant and stop for a break," Uncle Carl mumbled nervously.

"I thought we would all be dead by now," Mom whispered, breaking the silence.

"So did I," Grandma added. "God spared our lives. Let's bow our heads and thank Him for it." Then she prayed, "Thank you, dear Lord, for sparing our lives. Thank you! Thank you for watching over us. We praise you for protecting us. In Jesus name, Amen,"

I sat silently amazed that God had really spared our lives. It seemed like an unbelievable miracle. We survived!

Uncle Carl drove to the next restaurant and stopped. We all looked at the sides of the car for marks for it seemed the semis had surely touched it somewhere. No marks! Uncle Carl went into the restaurant to relax while the rest of us stayed in or around the car and ate a biscuit snack.

I had no desire to be cooped up in Uncle Carl's loaded, white capped, copper-bullet, station wagon flying down any highway with him behind the wheel again. I was thankful Grandma volunteered to drive for awhile. Later Uncle Carl drove seemingly with a bit more caution.

Within myself I quietly praised God for our survival and prayed for His continued protection and that this trip would end safe and soon. We were delivered. It seemed like a miracle. We all felt the death threat shake the car and thought it was our end. We were extremely thankful to be alive. How could I at that time ever dream I would later welcome death?

Leaving the colony behind was not my choice! Circumstances and people forced me out of the only home I had known for twelve years.

Where is God?

Appendix

Preparing to leave Elkhart for Lael Colony
Patricia with Fred before leaving the colony
Patricia the day before leaving the colony

```
#1 Exod-20:1-26 *       #2 Psa - 1:1-6          #3 Matt-19:16-21
   Exod-31:16-18            Psa -15:1-5             Mark-12:28-34
   Lev -20:22-26           Psa -19:1-14            John- 7:16,17,(38)
   Mala- 4:1-6             Psa -23:1-6             1-John-5:1-5,18,

#4 John-17:3,17 *       #5 Isa.-45:17,18 *      #6 Titus-1:2,16 *
   Deut-26:15-19           Psa -24:1-10            1-Cor-2:9,14
   Neh - 9:6               Psa -25:1-22            Rev - 2:7-11,
   Isa -57:15              Psa -68:1-4,32,         Rev -21:1-8
   1-Tim-6:11-16 *        Psa -75:5-7             Rev-22:1-21

#7 Exod-15:26           #8 Psa -78:1-7          #9 Matt- 7:12-14
   Exod-19:4-6             Psa-100:1-5             Luke-13:23-25
   Deut- 7:6,9            Psa-103:1-22            Isa -56:3-5
   Deut-10:12-17          Psa-105:1-15,43,        Isa -58:11-14
   Isa -26:1-4 *         Psa-136:1-26            Rev- 14:1-5,12,13
```

The Elder's "Nine Blocks"

On the plantation school's porch decades later

Other

Books

by

Patricia
Hochstetler

Patricia Hochstetler

Book One

Delusion

Growing Up
in an
Amish-Jewish Cult

Released June 2007

Why share
the pain?

Delusion is the story of one child, Patricia Hochstetler, caught in the trap of parental good intentions. Between the ages of four and six she was snatched from the warmth of *Jesus Loves Me* and thrust into a world that was cold and barren.

She wanted to please God and her parents, but the harder she tried the more desperate and confused she became. "Why is my aunt hiding out in the woods? Why did my cousin get taken out and dumped? Why is my father acting so strange? What can I do to be sure I'm going to heaven?" The unspoken questions, even of a child, could never be answered for no one dared question the rules.

The author reminds us that no one decides to join a *cult*. Parents set out to find truth, to draw closer to God. In their wayward search their children become scarred. Confusion reigns because the rules change for no apparent reason. If it was good yesterday, why is it bad today? Parents who blindly accept the word of a leader are dangerously close to being engulfed by a cult.

In *Delusion* we see how the trap was set for one little girl and her family. Her memories and family stories reveal how powerful the need to belong really is. It is a revelation of how much they were willing to surrender in order to be a part of the group. It happened right here in the United States! These family members were industrious, intelligent, compassionate, God-fearing people. But the lack of discernment brought broken relationships, heartache, despair, and even death.

Patricia Hochstetler is finally telling her story. This book is a glimpse of how easy it is to be drawn into the dangers and despair of a cult. This book is the first of a three-part series.

The next is *Deliverance.*

To be released in the Spring of 2008

After every storm there is the sunshine of a new day.

What happens after a "lifetime" as a caged bird? How long will it take for dependance on the cage to finally break free and the beauty of God's world and family become self-evident? These are questions we would all ask of anyone who survived such an unimaginable childhood.

Unfortunately there are very few out there who can answer these question positively. Patricia Hochstetler in her final book, *Deliverance,* shows how Christ walked in every footstep with her as she was truly led into her own spiritual healing.

Could any of us have done it? Yes. With Christ at our side all things are possible, even this.